An Introduction to WALL INSCRIPTIONS from Pompeii and Herculaneum

REX E. WALLACE

Bolchazy-Carducci Publishers, Inc.
Wauconda, Illinois USA

General editor:
Laurie Haight Keenan

An Introduction to Wall Inscriptions From Pompeii an Herculaneum
by Rex E. Wallace

Bolchazy-Carducci Publishers, Inc.
1000 Brown Street, Unit 101
Wauconda, Illinois 60084
www.bolchazy.com

ISBN 0-86516-570-X

Printed in the United States of America
by United Graphics
2005

Library of Congress Cataloging-in-Publication Data

Wallace, Rex.
An introduction to wall inscriptions from Pompeii and Herculaneum : introduction, inscriptions with notes, historical commentary, vocabulary / Rex E. Wallace.
p. cm.
Includes bibliographical references and index.
ISBN 0-86516-570-X (pbk. : alk. paper)
1. Inscriptions, Latin--Italy--Pompeii (Extinct city) 2. Inscriptions, Latin--Italy--Herculaneum (Extinct city) 3. Pompeii (Extinct city)--Antiquities. 4. Herculaneum (Extinct city)--Antiquities. I. Title.
CN533.W35 2003
937'.7--dc22

2003023037

CONTENTS

PREFACE

The aim of this text is to provide Latinists with a reasonably comprehensive introduction to wall inscriptions from the Campanian cities of Pompeii and Herculaneum. There is much to be learned about Latin and about the Roman world from these inscriptions, particularly the graffiti, of which a good portion was written by less educated members of society. In composing this book, I attempted to balance the needs of undergraduates with those of more advanced students. I also hope that classicists, historians and linguists, particularly Romance linguists, will find it a useful resource.

This text is organized into two parts. Part I is introductory material. This includes a short overview of inscriptions from Pompeii and Herculaneum, a more detailed discussion of wall inscriptions, and a description of orthographic and linguistic features characteristic of the dipinti and graffiti from these two cities. Part I concludes with a short bibliography. Part II is a selection of wall inscriptions from Pompeii and Herculaneum. A selection of facsimiles of dipinti and graffiti, a list of abbreviations used in the inscriptions, an index of proper names, and a list of vocabulary are located at the end of the text.

The inscriptions presented here were chosen in order to provide the reader with a representative selection of the different types of wall inscriptions that have been recovered at Pompeii and Herculaneum. The selection includes inscriptions that illustrate variation in the orthography, pronunciation, morphology and syntax of Latin during the first century AD. These features are attested with greater frequency in graffiti and for this reason I have included a greater number of this type of wall inscription in the text.

Translating wall inscriptions is not always as easy as it appears at first glance. This is particularly true of graffiti because it is often difficult, if not impossible, to reconstruct the contexts in which they were written, and also because orthography and grammar may diverge rather sharply from the literary norms to which most Latinists are accustomed. Accordingly, I have supplied notes and commentary as an aid to readers unfamiliar with the language of the inscriptions. All words used in the inscriptions are alphabetized in the Vocabulary. Proper names found in the wall inscriptions are given in an Index of Proper Names.

The final section of this text includes facsimiles of wall inscriptions. Mat Olkovikas, a former graduate student at the University of Massachusetts Amherst, copied, detailed and digitized the facsimiles from drawings published in the *Corpus Inscriptionum Latinarum*, Volume IV.

Many of the inscriptions in this text were field-tested in undergraduate and graduate classes that I taught at the University. I am especially grateful to the students who participated in my undergraduate seminar on Wall Inscriptions. They worked through large portions of the inscriptions and the commentary, and provided valuable feedback.

I thank Charles Babcock, Joe Eska, Gilbert Lawall, Willis Regier, George Ryan, and Maureen Ryan for comments on earlier versions of the text. I alone am responsible for any errors in the text, but there would have been many more had these folks not given generously of their time and expertise. I am indebted to Mat Olkovikas for cheerfully undertaking the task of preparing and editing the digital images of the facsimiles. I also thank Wendy Watkins, Curator of the Center of Epigraphical Studies at The Ohio State University, who helped me track down several articles on Pompeiian inscriptions. Finally, I wish to acknowledge the assistance of Katherine Hofmann and Bethanie Sawyer. During the final stages of editing and proofreading the text their keen eyes were invaluable.

Rex E. Wallace
University of Massachusetts Amherst
July 9, 2004

GRAMMATICAL ABBREVIATIONS

abl.	ablative
acc.	accusative
act.	active
adv.	adverb
cond.	conditional
conj.	conjunction
dat.	dative
dep.	deponent
fem.	feminine
fut.	future
gen.	genitive
impf.	imperfect
impv.	imperative
indecl.	indeclinable
indef. pron.	indefinite pronoun
inter. pron.	interrogative pronoun
masc.	masculine
neut.	neuter
nom.	nominative
num.	number
part.	particle
pass.	passive
perf.	perfect
pers. pro.	personal pronoun
pl.	plural
pres.	present
rel. adv.	relative adverb
rel. pron.	relative pronoun
sent.	sentence
sg.	singular
subj.	subjunctive

INTRODUCTION

§1. Inscriptions from Pompeii and Herculaneum

The ancient Roman cities of Pompeii and Herculaneum are two of the most abundant sources for Latin inscriptions. There are over 8,000 inscriptions incised or painted on the walls of homes, businesses, and public buildings in these two cities. If inscriptions on wax tablets and inscriptions incised on stone, ceramic, and metal are included in the count, the total is closer to 11,000. Most of these inscriptions are written in Latin, but there are also inscriptions in Etruscan, Greek, and Oscan. Thus, Pompeii and Herculaneum constitute one of classical antiquity's most precious epigraphic resources.

§1.1 Types of Inscriptions

Latin inscriptions from Pompeii and Herculaneum can be arranged into categories based on the function or purpose that they served and based on the material on which they were written.

The most familiar types of inscription at Pompeii and Herculaneum are those incised on stone. These were carved by professional stonecutters and were erected at public expense in order to commemorate the construction of public buildings, the careers of distinguished political figures, and so forth. Professional craftsmen also carved funerary inscriptions, especially those of prominent Pompeiians. These inscriptions were set up on funerary monuments in the necropolises located outside of the city gates.

One of the most important epigraphic finds at Pompeii was made in the house of a businessman named Lucius Caecilius Iucundus (V, 1, 26). In a wooden box stashed in the atrium Iucundus had stored 153 receipts of business transactions. These were incised in cursive style on wooden tablets whose writing surface was coated, in most cases, with a thin layer of a wax-like substance (hence the label, wax tablets). These tablets, together with those from Herculaneum and those recently discovered in a luxury hospitality center located just south of Pompeii in Agro Murecine, are invaluable for the study of business and economy at Pompeii.

Other types of inscription, including those incised, painted, or impressed on amphoras and ceramics of various styles, and on tiles and metal objects, also had commercial functions. They were used to facilitate accounting, to label commercial goods, or to indicate ownership of pottery and other objects of everyday use.

The most abundant types of inscriptions found at Pompeii and Herculaneum, making up nearly three quarters of the total number of inscriptions from these sites, are the so-called *inscriptiones parietariae* 'inscriptions on walls.'

§1.2 Wall Inscriptions

Wall inscriptions were either incised by means of a stylus or some other type of sharp implement or they were painted. The former are known as graffiti, the latter are dipinti.

Dipinti include advertisements of various types, of which the most important are *programmata,* announcements endorsing the candidacies of politicians in municipal elections, and *edicta munerum,* announcements of gladiatorial contests. They also include a small number of salutations and communications of a more public nature. These inscriptions were generally placed in prominent locations because they were intended to be read by the literate public.

In contrast to dipinti, graffiti were spontaneous and unauthorized writings (and drawings) on the walls of private and public buildings. A significant segment of the corpus consisted of names, but there was also much humor, tidbits of popular wisdom, obscenities, historical references, and even some homespun philosophizing. Graffiti from Pompeii and Herculaneum are invaluable as sources of information about the daily activities, the attitudes and the language of the working classes in these cities.

§1.3 Dipinti

Electoral Announcements or *Programmata*

The most important types of advertisement, and the most numerous, are those in support of political candidates. Some 2,600 have survived. They give the names of well over a hundred candidates and the political offices for which they were standing.

Electoral announcements or *programmata* were usually painted upon the sides of walls along well-traveled streets or on the tomb monuments that lined the roads leading up to the gates of the city. Most were painted in a bright red color, but a few were painted in black, after the walls had been given a fresh coat of whitewashing.

A large part of the surviving electoral announcements, those known as *programmata recentiores,* can be dated to the period AD 50–79, with most of those belonging to the final years of the city, AD 62–79. Interestingly, however, a few *programmata* have survived, primarily those painted directly on unplastered walls, that can be dated to the final decades of the Republican period, e.g., I, 1, 1). These inscriptions, known as *programmata antiquissima,* cover a chronological span of about 50 years, roughly 80–30 BC. Very few can be assigned to the period 30 BC–AD 50.

The most recent electoral announcements, in particular those composed in the period relatively close to the eruption of Vesuvius, were painted by professional sign-painters in a well-developed calligraphic style known as *scripta actuaria* (for examples, see Facsimiles, nos. 1–4). The organizational layout of these inscriptions also shows considerable care. The names of the candidates and the office for which they were standing were prominently presented, and the inscriptions generally had an aesthetically pleasing appearance.

Candidates at Pompeii (we have no information for Herculaneum, but see III, 1, 1 and III, 1, 2) ran for one of two political offices. The senior office was referred to as the duumvirate. A pair of **duumvirī** (also **duovirī**) who had the official title of **duumvirī iūre dīcundō**, 'duumvirs for administering justice,' (commonly abbreviated **IIvir i d** or **d i d**) held his office. In addition to judicial functions, the duumvirs were responsible for the public finances of the city, for proceedings in the **ordō dēcuriōnum**, 'town council,' and for elections in the **comitium**, 'assembly.' Every fifth year duumvirs with greater responsibilities were selected. These duumvirs were known as **quinquennālēs**, 'quinquennial duumvirs,' and they were obligated to take a census of all citizens and to revise the list of members in the town's council. Two officers known as **aedīlēs** held the junior office. The aediles were responsible for maintenance of public roads and of public and sacred buildings, regulation of the markets and of public land. Both offices were held for a single year, and a candidate had to serve as an aedile before he could stand for the duumvirate. And a candidate had to wait five years before standing again for the senior political office.

The content of *programmata* was concise and to the point. They began with the name of the candidate in the accusative case. The political office for which the candidate was standing, also in the accusative case and almost always abbreviated, followed. The verb phrase **ovf** or **o · v · f**, an abbreviation for **ōrō vōs faciātis**, 'I entreat you to vote for,' whose final verb **faciātis** governs the name of the candidate and the political office for which he was standing, was placed after the accusative noun phrases. The following is a typical example (see Facsimile 1).

(1) 7204; I, vii, 1; Via dell' Abbondanza.

C · I · Polybium
IIvir · ovf

I entreat you to elect Gaius Iulius Polybius as duumvir (the highest political office in Pompeii).

The candidates were often given attributes from a short list of stock epithets. These descriptive phrases were in the accusative case and thus in apposition to the name of the candidate. Some common phrases, many of which were abbreviated, were: **v · b** = **virum bonum**, 'a man of good standing (in the community),' **d · r · p** = **dignum reī pūblicae**, 'worthy of public office,' **bene mer** = **bene merentem**, 'well-deserving,' **iuvenem probum**, 'an honorable man,' etc. It was also common for the short sentence **dignus est** (or an abbreviated variant), 'He is worthy (of public office),' to be appended to the recommendation even though in many cases it was redundant, repeating in a general way what was already indicated by **d · r · p**. The following inscription is a good example (see Facsimile 2).

(2) 7208; I, vii, 1; Via dell' Abbondanza.

1 **P · Paquium**
2 **Proculum · II · vir · d · r · p · ovf**
3 **dignus · est**

I entreat you to elect Publius Paquius Proculus as duumvir, (a man) worthy of public office. He is worthy.

Often, the name of the person, of the trade or craft association, or of the sporting or religious society, that supported the candidacy was written at the end of an electoral announcement. The name of the supporter or group of supporters — the so-called **rogātor** or **rogātōrēs** — was in the nominative case, and this was usually followed by the appropriate form of the verb **rogō, rogāre**, 'to ask (someone) to elect,' again usually abbreviated. In the following example, an association of 'fruit-vendors', **pomārī**, supported the candidate Marcus Holconius Priscus (see Facsimile 3).

(3) 202, add. pg. 203; VI, viii, 14 or 21; Via di Mercurio.

1 **M Holconium**
2 **Priscum · IIvir · i · d ·**
3 **pomari · universi**
4 **cum · Helvio · Vestale · rog**

All of the fruit-vendors together with Helvius Vestalis ask you to elect Marcus Holconius Priscus as duumvir for the administration of justice.

Most *programmata* presented the name of a single candidate, but there were a few, such as the following, which gave the names of two candidates standing for office. Very few *programmata* contained a full slate of candidates (see I, 1, 11).

(4) 7488; II, iv, 1; Via dell' Abbondanza.

A · Trebium · Valentem
et · Cn · Audium · Bassum
d · v · i · d · quinq · ovf

I ask (you) to elect Aulus Trebius Valens and Gnaeus Audius Bassus as duumviri quinquinales for the administration of justice.

Occasionally, *programmata* diverged dramatically from the norm. A few were composed in poetic meter. One of the best examples is *CIL* IV.6626, cited in (5) below, which was written in an elegaic couplet (for discussion of the metrical peculiarities, see I, 1, 42):

(5) 6626; V, iv, a; Vicolo di M. Lucretius Fronto.

si · pudor · in vita quicquam · prodesse · putatur
Lucretius · hic · Fronto · dignus · honore · bono · est

If decency is considered to have any value in life, this (man), Lucretius Fronto, is worthy of high esteem/high public office.

One of the most distinctive features of *programmata*, and of advertisements in general, was the number of abbreviations that were employed. As the *programmata* cited above show, the office for which the candidate was standing, as well as any epithets attributed to the candidate, could be and usually were abbreviated. In some cases, as in (6) below (= I, 1, 28), even the name of the candidate, if it was particularly well known, could be abbreviated. But it was typically the case that the most prominent aspects of the electoral advertisement were written in full, viz., the name (*nomen* and/or *cognomen*) of the candidate and the name (*nomen* or *cognomen*) of the supporter, while the formulaic material — repeated in advertisement after advertisement — was abbreviated.

(6) 1048; I, iv, 19–20; Via dell'Abbondanza.

Q · P · P · iuvenem

2 aed · ovf · d · r · p
3 Sabinus · rog · copo

I entreat you to elect Quintus Paquius Proculus as aedile, (a man) worthy of public office. Sabinus, the innkeeper, requests (this).

Edicta Munerum or Gladiatorial Announcements

The other major type of advertisement was for gladiatorial games. A large portion of these inscriptions come from areas adjacent to the amphitheatre, including the necropolis located outside the city beyond the Porta Nocera, or from the theatre district. The remaining inscriptions of this type were found along the major streets in the other districts of the city such as the Via di Nola. Like *programmata,* these inscriptions followed a standard organizational format. The main ingredients included the name of the sponsor of the gladiatorial show, the number of pairs of gladiators who were scheduled to fight, and a list of amenities to be offered, such as awnings to shield spectators from the sun. Like any informative playbill, these advertisements also gave the dates of the shows, where they were to take place, and, in some cases, under what circumstances, e.g., in honor of an emperor. *CIL* IV.7992 is representative (for this text and notes, see I, 2, 64; Facsimile 4).

(7) 3884; IX, viii, 4; Via di Nola.

1 D · Lucreti ·
2 Satri · Valentis · flaminis · Neronis · Caesaris · Aug fili
3 perpetui · gladiatorum · paria · XX · et · D · Lucreti{o} · Valentis fili
4 glad · paria · X · pug · Pompeis · VI · V · IV · III · pr · Idus Apr · venatio · legitima ·
5 et · vela · erunt
6 scr
7 Aemilius
8 Celer sing
9 ad luna
10 scr
11 Celer

> Twenty pairs of gladiators of Decimus Lucretius Satrius Valens, permanent flamen (priest) of Nero Caesar, the son of Augustus, and ten pairs of gladiators of Decimus Lucretius, the son of Valens, will fight at Pompeii on the sixth, fifth, fourth, third day, and on the day before the Ides of April (April 8, 9, 10, 11, 12). There will be the customary beast hunt and awnings. Aemilius Celer paints (this) alone by moonlight. Celer paints (this).

As was the case with *programmata, edicta munera* also make use of abbreviatory conventions. In the inscription cited above, the main verb **pugn** and the phrase indicating the date of the games **pr Idus Apr** were abbreviated. **pugn** stood for **pugnābunt** and **pr Idus Apr** stood for **prīdiē Īdūs Aprīlēs**. Numbers were never spelled out in these inscriptions, but were always indicated by ciphers.

Other types of advertisements

In addition to the two major categories of dipinti, a handful of other epigraphical types survived. Public acclamations and salutations, most of which were in honor of the emperor (e.g., I, 5, 84) or other popular personalities such as the sponsors of gladiatorial contests (e.g., I, 5, 85), are two minor types of dipinti, as are advertisements for rental properties (e.g., I, 4, 78) and notices of items lost and found (e.g., I, 4, 82).

§1.4 Graffiti

Graffiti make up the largest segment of wall inscriptions at Pompeii and Herculaneum, numbering over 5,000. They were inscribed in almost every imaginable location: on exterior walls of homes and businesses; on the interior walls of homes, in reception rooms, bedrooms, storage rooms, and peristyles; in public baths and latrines; in brothels; in the archways leading between the theatres; in passageways leading into the amphitheatre; on the columns of the public exercise areas; and on facades of sepulchral monuments. They covered a considerable range of topics or themes, from the philosophical and the poetic to the lewd and the obscene.

The simplest graffiti recorded the names of individuals. The following name was incised on the wall of a tablinum:

(8) 1530; V, ii, b; Via degli Scienziati.

Successus

A resident of Puteoli, perhaps in Pompeii on business, incised his name on a pilaster separating the facades of two houses:

(9) 1472; VI, x, 3–4; Via della Fortuna.

M · Verrius · Quirinalis · Puteolanus

Marcus Verrius Quirinalis from Puteoli.

Several inscriptions included the verb phrase **hic fuit**, 'was here.' This phrase gives the text a contemporary feel, for this is one type of graffiti that is ubiquitous today at tourist destinations throughout the States and Europe. The following is an inscription that refers to a famous mime who performed regularly in Pompeii:

(10) 1305; VI, ix, 5; Via di Mercurio.

Paris · hic
fuit

Paris was here.

Another common type of graffito, consisting of individual names, was the greeting or salutation directed to friends or to family. The name of the person or persons who received the saluation was in the dative case and the name of the person who was responsible for the communication was in the nominative, but there were many variations on this formula. In *CIL* IV.4100, cited below, a laundry man by the name of **Crēscēns** gave a greeting to a **cōpō** or 'innkeeper.' Note that the word for 'greeting,' **sal**, was abbreviated (= **salūtem**) and that the verb **dīcit**, which governed this noun, had to be supplied from the context.

(11) 4100; V, ii, 4; Via di Nola.

fullo
Cresces
coponi sal

The fuller, Crescens, (expresses, gives) a greeting to the innkeeper.

Soldiers who were stationed at or near Pompeii inscribed their names and the number of their cohort and century on the walls of houses where they were boarded. The following was incised on a column in the atrium of a *domus* located at VIII, iii, 21. Note, once again, the abbreviations (**Sex** = **Sextus**; **coh** = **cohortis**; **pr** = **praetōriānae**; **c** = **centuriōnis**).

(12) 1994; VIII, iii, 21; Via della Scuola.

Sex · Decimius · Rufus
milis · coh · V · pr · c · Martialis

Sextus Decimus Rufus, soldier of the fifth praetorian cohort, of the century of Martialis.

Section §1.3 above described advertisements for gladiatorial shows. In addition to this type of inscription, there were numerous graffiti recording the names of gladiators, some of whom, to judge from the content of the inscriptions, achieved considerable popularity. Consider the graffito of a gladiator by the name of **Celadus**, who was the object of adoration of young Pompeiian women.

(13) 4397; V, v, 3; Via di Nola.

suspirium
puellarum
Celadus Tr

Heartthrob of young women, Celadus, the Thracian.

Some gladiatorial graffiti were modeled on **libellī munerāriī**, programs or playbills that listed the pairings for gladiatorial combats. This type of inscription gave the names of the combatants and indicated who was victorious and who was vanquished. It was sometimes accompanied by a crude drawing depicting the gladiatorial combat. This type of graffito also had statistics on the combatant's record in the arena, e.g., the total number of fights, total number of victories earned, and so forth. A typical example is *CIL* IV.10236, cited below (Facsimile 5). This graffito was inscribed over a drawing of two gladiators. The gladiator on the left side stands poised to strike, while the gladiator on the right is kneeling, or falling, to the ground. The abbreviation **c** stood for **corōnārum**, the 'victory crowns' awarded for an outstanding performance in the arena. The abbreviations **v** and **m** stood for **vīcit**, 'he won,' and **missus est**, 'he was pardoned,' respectively.

(14) 10236; necropolis, Porta di Nocera; Via di Nocera.

1	**M Att**	**L Raecius Felix**
2	**M · Attilius I c I**	**XII c XII · m**
3	**v**	

Marcus Attilius Marcus Attilius 1 fight, 1 victory crown he won	Lucius Raecius Felix 12 fights, 12 victory crowns, he was pardoned

Arguably, the most notable segment of graffiti from Pompeii and Herculaneum is the one that may be characterized as amatory in theme or topic. Some of these inscriptions are worthy of mention not only because of their sentiments, but also because they were written in poetic meters. The following poem (see Facsimile 6), which was incised on the wall in the home of Lucius Caecilius Iucundus (for whom, see above §1.1), is a good example because it expresses an idea that was quite popular at Pompeii and Herculaneum, and one that was often repeated in wall inscriptions.

The meter of the inscription is the elegaic couplet (though there are some metrical irregularites, for which see II, 7, 129).

(15) 4091; V, i, 23–26; Via Stabiana.

quis amat valeat pereat qui
nescit amare bis tanto pereat
quisquis amare vetat

Whoever loves, may he fare well. May he perish who does not know how to love. May he perish by twice as much, whoever forbids (someone) to love.

Other inscriptions belonging to this category are appealing because of the modern, romantic note that they strike. *CIL* IV.2146 is a graffito incised by a visitor to Pompeii who spent the night alone in an inn pining for his woman.

(16) 2146; VII, xii, 35; Vicolo di Eumachia.

Vibius Restitutus hic
solus · dormivit et Urbanam
suam desiderabat

Vibius Restitutus slept here alone and he kept longing for his Urbana.

Metrical inscriptions with amatory themes were common at Pompeii, but there were also metrical inscriptions on other topics. For example, the following poem, written in dactylic pentameters, expressed the theme of the ephemeral nature of life (see Facsimile 7).

(17) 9123; IX, xiii, 4; Via dell' Abbondanza.

nihil durare potest tempore perpetuo
cum bene sol nituit redditur Oceano
decrescit Phoebe quae modo plena fuit

ven[to]rum feritas saepe fit aura levis

Nothing is able to endure for an everlasting period of time (= forever). When the sun has shone radiantly, it returns to the Ocean. Phoebe (the moon), which a little while ago was full, wanes. The fierceness of the winds often becomes a gentle breeze.

Graffiti also provide us with interesting glimpses into commercial activity in the city. Memoranda of accounts listing ingredients purchased and their cost were occasionally scratched on the walls of businesses. The following example comes from a bakery in the neighborhood of the Stabian gate. The memorandum reads as follows:

(18) 4000; I, iii, 27; Vicolo di Tesmo.

oleum l a IV
palea a V
faenum a XVI
diaria a V
furfure a VI
viria I a [–]
oleum a VI

Oil, 1 pound for 4 *asses*; straw for 5 *asses*; hay for 16 *asses*; a day's wages for 5 *asses*; bran for 6 *asses*; 1 necklace for 3 *asses*; oil for 6 *asses*.

Individuals also occasionally made a note of a business transaction by writing it on the wall of their homes. The following is a memorandum noting the date of the purchase or the receipt of a tunic and its cost. The symbol * was used to represent the word **dēnārius**.

(19) 1392; VI, xi, 16; Via del Labirinto.

III Idus Apriles
tunica * I

A tunic for one *dēnārius* on the third day before the Ides of April (April 11).

Others incised notices of goods and services for sale. For example, the following graffito, advertising the sale of manure and a wheel, was incised on the wall near the Porta Marina.

(20) 1754, add. pg. 211, ind. pg. 790; Via di Marina.

Eupemus
stecus e fundo · et
rota

Eupemus (is selling) manure from the farm and a potter's wheel.

Occasionally, students composed graffiti. There are many examples of abecedaria (see Facsimile 8), both in Latin and in Greek, incised by those who were practicing or perhaps showing off their skill at writing their abc's. Sometimes the alphabets were written in reverse order, and sometimes they were written by alternating one letter from the beginning and then one letter from the end of the alphabet, e.g., **AXBVCT**, etc. Exercises such as these must have been employed in school to help students master the alphabet.

Quotations from Roman poets who were studied in school, most prominently from Vergil, are also found. For example, the first line of the *Aeneid* appears several times, as do the opening words of Lucretius' *De Rerum Natura*. An interesting graffito, cited below (21), was probably used as a model for students who were learning to master the metrical structure of hexameter verse.

(21) 4235; V, ii, 1; Via di Nola.

barbara barbaribus barbabant barbara barbis

Graffiti referring to specific historical events were not all that common at Pompeii. However, one event was referred to in several graffiti, *viz.*, the riot in the amphitheatre in AD 59. We learn from the historian Tacitus (*Annales*, XIV.17) that fans from Pompeii and rival fans from Nuceria came to blows in the amphitheatre at Pompeii during a gladiatorial contest. The fighting escalated into a full-fledged riot in which many Nucerians lost their lives. The violence was so terrible that the Roman Senate was called in to investigate, and gladiatorial combats were prohibited at Pompeii for a period of ten years, although this order was apparently rescinded in AD 62, thanks to the intervention of Nero's wife Poppaea, a native of Pompeii. The following graffito refers to the plight of the Nucerians and the impact of the loss of the gladiatorial contest on the inhabitants of the area.

(22) 1293; VI, ix, 6–7; Via di Mercurio.

Campani victoria una
cum Nucerinis peristis

O Campanians, with this victory you've been destroyed along with the Nucerians.

No discussion of the types of graffiti found at Pompeii and Herculaneum would be complete without citing what may well be the most well known graffito from this area (see Facsimile 9). Some clever person, lamenting the vast amounts of graffiti that covered the walls of the city, wrote the following (see II, 9, 185 for discussion):

(23) 2487; II, 7; Amphitheatre.

ad · miror te · paries · non c[e]cidisse
qui tot · scriptorum taedia sustineas

O wall, I am amazed that you have not fallen down since you support the loathsome scribblings of so many writers.

While we can understand the sentiments of the writer, at the same time we are grateful to those who have, by means of their scribblings, provided us with an invaluable means for gaining insight into the affairs and the language of the inhabitants of Pompeii and Herculaneum in the first century AD.

§2. The Language of Wall Inscriptions

The Latin of the wall inscriptions from Pompeii and Herculaneum is distinct from the Latin of Roman authors such as Cicero, Caesar, Horace, and Vergil in important respects. Whereas the Latin of these authors reflects a tradition of carefully crafted literary composition, based on Latin as it was spoken by educated (and therefore in large part) aristocratic Romans, the language of wall inscriptions, particularly the graffiti, reflects the Latin of less educated social orders (working classes, slaves, freedmen, etc.) as it was used during the first century AD. This variety of Latin is generally known as 'Vulgar' Latin, a label derived from the Latin adjective **vulgāris, -e** meaning 'of the common people.'

In the sections that follow, features of orthography and grammar that occurred frequently in graffiti from Pompeii and Herculaneum are discussed. For a more comprehensive discussion of these features, and of other features associated with non-literary Latin, refer to section §4.5 of the bibliography located at the end of the Introduction.

§2.1 Orthography and Phonology

Long Vowels

In Latin orthography long vowels and short vowels were generally not written in a distinctive manner. In dipinti, however, particularly *programmata* and *edicta munerum*, long vowels were sometimes indicated by means of apices (**á**) written over vowel letters (**á, é, ó, ú**). The long vowel **ī** was spelled sometimes by means of I-*longa*. In the standard form, the letter extended well above the average height of other letters in the inscription, e.g., **universI**, 'all,' nom. pl. masc. A second form of I-*longa* had a long coda or tail, which extended well below the imaginary bottom line of the inscription, and was represented in transcription by the letter **j**, e.g., **domj**, 'home,' loc. sg. fem. Long **ī** was also spelled by the digraph **ei**, e.g., **veivant** = **vīvant**, 'may they live,' 3rd pl. pres.

subj. act.; **Sabeinum** = **Sabīnum**, cognomen, acc. sg. masc.; **Eidus**, 'Ides,' acc. pl. fem.; **seiquis**, 'if anyone,' cond. conj. + indef. pro., nom. pl. masc.

In this text, apices over vowels are not indicated, nor is I-*longa*, but the spelling **ei** = **ī** is kept and words with this spelling feature are identified in the notes.

Contraction

Contraction of **iī** and **ii** to **ī** was the rule for wall inscriptions from Pompeii and Herculaneum. In fact, in the entire corpus of wall inscriptions from these two cities, only a few words preserved this sequence in uncontracted form, e.g., **iūdiciīs**, 'decisions,' dat. pl. neut. of **iūdicium**. This feature affected the case forms in first and second declension nouns and adjectives ending in **-ia** and **-ius**. The nominative plural and the dative/ablative plural of second declension nouns and adjectives in **-ius** were regularly written as **ī**, which represented a contraction of the short **i**-vowel of the stem and the long **ī**-vowel of the ending. The dative/ablative plural of first declension nominals in **-ia** was regularly written **-īs**, which also represented a contraction of the short vowel of the stem and the long vowel of the ending. Examples are: **pomārī**, 'fruit-sellers,' nom. pl. masc. of **pomārius**; **praedīs**, 'property,' abl. pl. neut. of **praedium**. Contraction was also regular for verb forms, especially for perfect tense forms of compounds of the verb 'go,' which had the sequences **iī** and **ii**. Examples are: **pereit** = **perīt**, 'he died,' 3rd sg. perf. act., cf. **periit**; **redei** = **redī**, 'I returned,' 1st sg. perf. act., cf. **rediī**; **fastidī** = **fastidiī**, 'I scorned,' 1st sg. perf. act.

Nota Bene: The regular form of the genitive singular of second declension nominals in **-ius** and **-ium** was **-ī**, not **-iī**, down through the Augustan period. By the end of the first century AD genitives in **-ī** were being replaced by genitives in **-iī**, with the **-i** of the stem appearing due to analogy with other case forms. See §2.2 Declension, Second Declension Genitive Singular.

Monophthongization of ae and au

The diphthong **ae** was monophthongized in the speech of some Pompeiians to a long, open, mid-vowel [ɛ:] (a vowel similar in quality to the one in English *bed*), which was spelled by **ē**. Monophthongization of **ae** is particularly well attested in final syllables, where it had an impact on the shape of first declension inflectional endings. Thus, in some wall inscriptions, particularly graffiti, the ending of the genitive, dative, and locative singular and of the nominative plural of first declension nouns was spelled as **ē**, rather than as **ae**. Examples are: **Cesernīnē**, cognomen, dat. sg. fem., cf. **Cesernīnae**; **Putiolānē**, 'of Puteoli,' dat. sg. fem., cf. **Putiolānae**; **Successē**, cognomen, dat. sg. fem., cf. **Successae**.

Hypercorrect spellings, in which the digraph **ae** was used to spell long **ē**, are found in a handful of words, e.g., **aegisse** for expected **ēgisse**, perf. act. inf. of **agō**, 'to drive, lead.' Interestingly, the digraph **ae** was used more frequently to spell a short **e**, which is understandable because short **e** in Latin had the same quality, namely [ɛ], as the product of the monophthongization of **ae**, which was [ɛ:], e.g., **Graphicae** for **Graphice**, voc. sg. masc. of the cognomen **Graphicus**; and note **laesaerit** for **laeserit**, 'will have damaged,' 3rd sg. fut. perf. act. Pompeiian **laesaerit** may spell [lɛ:sɛrɪt] phonetically.

The monophthongization of **au** to **ō** was less common than the monophthongization of **ae** to **ē**, but enough examples exist to suggest that this diphthong too had become a long vowel, at least for some Pompeiian speakers. Examples are: **Clōdī**, gentilicium, voc. sg. masc., cf. **Claudius**, nom. sg. masc.; **cōpō**, 'inn-keeper,' nom. sg. masc., cf. **caupō**, nom. sg. masc.; **cōliclo,** 'cabbage,' acc. sg. neut., cf. **cauliculum**, nom. sg. neut.; **cōdātīs**, 'provided with tails' = 'followers,' abl. pl. masc., cf. **cauda**, 'tail.' Note also **plōstrārī**, 'wagoneers,' nom. pl. masc., cf. **plaustrum**, 'wagon.' In this word, however, **ō** is original and the diphthong **au** a hyperurbanism.

Short i and u in Medial Syllables

The spelling of the short high vowel in open medial syllables, especially before labial consonants **p**, **b**, **m**, fluctuated between **u** and **i** in Pompeiian speech. In some cases the vowel **u** was written in words where **i** was the standard spelling in classical Latin. Examples are: **optume**, 'best,' voc. sg. masc.; **optumē**, adv., to which one can compare **optimōs**, acc. pl. masc.; **maxu[mum]**, 'greatest,' nom. sg. neut., cf. **maximē**; **manuplōs**, 'infantry units,' acc. pl. masc., cf. **manipulōs**; **lacrumae**, 'tears,' nom. pl. fem., cf. **lacrimae**.

Short i in Final Syllables

In graffiti the short vowel **e** was used with considerable frequency for original short **i** in word-final syllables, e.g., **pugnābet**, 'will fight,' 3rd sg. fut. act., cf. **pugnābit**. An important result of this change was that present tense forms and future tense forms of 3rd conjugation verbs were indistinguishable in spelling in the second and third singular, e.g., **bibes**, 2nd sg. pres. act. (= **bibis**), vs. **bibes**, 2nd sg. fut. act. (= **bibēs**). Second and third conjugation forms in the second singular active and the third singular active were also spelled in the same way, e.g., second conjugation **mones** (= **monēs**) vs. third conjugation **deduces** (= **dēdūcis**). Examples of **e** for short **i** in third conjugation verbs are: **dēdūces**, 'lead away,' 2nd sg. pres. act., cf. **dēdūcis**; **vedes**, 'you sell,' 2nd sg. pres. act., cf. **vendis**.

There were a few examples of hypercorrect spellings, in which the letter **i** was used for original **e**, e.g., **mīlis**, 'soldier,' nom. masc. sg. for expected **mīles**, though other explanations for the final **i** here are possible (e.g., by analogy after other case forms, such as the genitive singular **mīlitis**, where **i** was regular).

Vocalic Hiatus

Original **e** that was in hiatus before another vowel was commonly spelled by **i**. Examples of this spelling were particularly common in graffiti in adjective forming suffixes such as **-eus**, 'made of,' and in second conjugation verb forms where original long **ē** was shortened to **e** before another vowel (*vocalis ante vocalem corripitur*), e.g., **moneō** vs. **monēs**. This change had the effect of eliminating distinctions between adjective suffixes such that the suffixes **-ius**, 'belonging to,' and **-eus**, 'made of,' were both spelled as **-ius**, e.g., **aēnia**, 'made of bronze,' nom. fem. sg., cf. **aēnea**. Second conjugation, third **i**-stem conjugation (**capiō**), and fourth conjugation presents had the same forms in the first and third persons singular of the indicative active, the first person of the present passive, and in all persons and numbers of the subjunctive, e.g., second conjugation **(h)abiō**, 'I hold,' vs. third conjugation **capiō**, 'I seize,' and fourth conjugation **audiō**, 'I hear'; **habiās** vs. **capiās, audiās**, etc. This feature was also found in the subjunctive forms of the verb 'go.' For example, in the first plural of the subjunctive, the Pompeiian form **iāmus**, 'let's go,' 1st pl. pres. subj., corresponded to the classical form **eāmus**. Hypercorrect spellings, in which **e** was used to spell original **i**, were also found, though infrequently: **moreor**, 'I die,' 1st sg. pres., cf. **morior**; **pateor**, 'I endure,' 1st sg. pres., cf. **patior**.

Some evidence suggests that original **i** in hiatus before another vowel turned into its consonantal counterpart and was pronounced as **y**, at least by some Pompeiians. Metrical evidence provides the clearest evidence for this proposal. I, 7, 97 (= *CIL* IV.813) scans as a hexameter if the first word **ōtiōsīs**, 'idle, at liesure,' dat. pl. masc., is trisyllabic, that is, scans as **ōtyōsīs**, with **i** in hiatus pronounced as a **y**. Similarly, *CIL* IV.1891 scans as a hexameter if the name **Theorianis** is trisyllabic, viz., **Theoryānīs**, with synizesis of **eo** and with **i** in hiatus before another vowel pronounced as **y**. It is worth noting that sporadic examples of this change are found even in literary Latin, as for example at Vergil *Aeneid* 2, 16, where the noun **abiete** must scan as trisyllabic and antepenultimate **i** must be pronounced as consonantal **y**, i.e., **abyete**.

Syncope of short vowels

The loss of short vowels in open medial syllables is well attested in wall inscriptions, particularly graffiti. In most cases vowels were lost when they stood next to nasals (**m**, **n**) or liquids (**l**, **r**), as in **domnus**, 'master,' which corresponds to unsyncopated **dominus**; and **suspendre**, 'to hang,' which corresponds to unsyncopated **suspendere**. But there are also cases where vowels were lost in other environments, as in **postas**, 'put,' acc. sg. fem., past participle of **pōnō**, cf. **positās**, and **frīdam**, 'cold water,' acc. sg. fem. of the adjective **frīgidus, -a, -um** (via **frīyidam**). Syncope was more common in syllables that immediately followed the accent, but **Herclanio**, 'at Herculaneum,' for **Herculāneō**, and **cubiclārius**, 'chamber-servant,' for **cubiculārius**, show that vowels in the syllable before the accent could also be syncopated.

In graffiti **i** in the third singular perfect active ending **-avit** was sometimes lost. Loss of **i** in **-āvit** yielded a third singular ending with the form **-aut** or, with change of word-final **-t** to **-d** (on which, see below, **Word-final Consonants**), **-aud**. The loss of **i** in this position was likely the result of a special kind of syncope restricted to the sequence -**āvi**. An example of a perfect with a syncopated third singular ending is **aberaut**, 'has lost,' 3rd sg. perf. act., cf. **aberrāvit**.

h

h at the beginning of words was lost in most dialects of Latin in the Republican period, but it was retained in the Latin of the educated, perhaps in part due to spelling pronunciations. In wall inscriptions **h** was not written in many native Latin words and it was not written in many words borrowed from Greek. Examples are: **ōra**, 'hour,' acc. sg. fem.; **abiat**, 'let him have,' 3rd sg. pres. subj., cf. **habeat**; **Ermorius**, cognomen, voc. sg. masc., cf. **Hermorius**. The absence of **h** for many speakers at Pompeii is further indicated by words in which **h** was written but where it had no etymological support. Examples are: **honerāta**, 'burdened,' acc. sg. fem., cf. **onerātam**; **hīre**, 'to go,' pres. inf., cf. **īre**; **havē**, 'fare well,' 2nd sg. impv., cf. **avē**.

b and v

v: In word-initial position the semi-vowel [w], spelled **v**, was pronounced by some Pompeiians as a bilabial fricative [β], a sound similar to that found medially in Spanish words such as **saber**, 'to know.' This pronunciation led to the spelling of **v** by means of the letter **b**, which more closely approximated the bilabial pronunciation of the consonant in this position. All of the examples are in graffiti: **Bērus**, cognomen, nom. sg. masc., cf. **Vērus**; **baliat**, 'may he fare well,' 3rd sg. pres. subj., cf. **valeat**; **benī**, 'come!,' 2nd sg. impv., cf. **venī**; **vāsia**, 'kisses,' acc. pl. neut., cf. **bāsia**.

b: In intervocalic position, the letter **v** was used to spell original **b**, albeit infrequently, e.g., **Vivī**, gentilicium, voc. sg. masc., cf.

Vibī; **Vivia**, gentilicium, nom. sg. fem., cf. **Vibia**; **tivi**, 'to you,' dat. sg. masc., cf. **tibi**. The spelling of original **b** by means of **v** indicated a fricative pronunciation, most likely a bilabial [β].

Thus, for some speakers at Pompeii, word-initial **v** [w] was changing to a fricative [β], and medial **b** [b] was changing also to a fricative [β].

Nasal + Stop Consonant

The nasals **m** and **n** were lost before the stop consonants (**p, b, t, d, c, g**) in the speech of some Pompeiian speakers. This feature was more common in graffiti than dipinti. The loss of the nasal was probably accompanied by nasalization of the preceding vowel. Examples are: **vedes**, 'you sell,' 2nd sg. pres. act., cf. **vendis**; **medācia**, 'lies,' acc. pl. neut., cf. **mendācia**; **Nypē**, cognomen, nom. sg. fem. (with Greek inflection), cf. **Nymphē**.

ns

The nasal **n** was regularly omitted before **s** in Pompeiian graffiti. This spelling points to the loss of the nasal, most likely with accompanying nasalization and lengthening of the preceding vowel. Omission of **n** before **s** was common also in Old Latin inscriptions. Thus the classical Latin spelling **ns** probably does not accurately reflect pronunciation. Examples are: **omnipotēs**, 'all-powerful,' voc. sg. masc., cf. **omnipotēns**; **quōservis**, 'fellow-servant,' nom. masc. sg., cf. **cōnservis**; **proficiscēs**, 'set out,' masc. nom. sg. pres. participle, cf. **proficiscēns**; **libēs**, 'willingly,' adv., cf. **lībēns**; **Crēscēs**, cognomen, nom. sg. masc., cf. **Crēscēns**; **Prudēs**, cognomen, nom. sg. masc., cf. **Prudēns**. Hypercorrect spellings, in which **n** was written before **s**, were not infrequent. Examples are: **Gangēns**, cognomen, nom. sg. masc., cf. **Gangēs**; **formōnsiōrem**, 'more handsome,' acc. sg. masc., cf. **formōsiōrem**; **pariēns**, 'wall,' nom. sg. fem., cf. **pariēs**.

Word-final Consonants

m: The omission of word-final **m** was a feature characteristic of all varieties of Latin. We know from Latin metrics that word-final **m** was not pronounced when the next word began with a vowel.

Presumably, then, despite the fact that final **m** is spelled in literary Latin, it was not pronounced. In Latin final **-Vm** was probably a long, possibly nasalized, vowel.

At Pompeii and Herculaneum final **m** was commonly written in dipinti, which is to be expected since this style of writing adhered more closely to spellings used by the educated classes. However, in graffiti, word-final **m** was commonly omitted. Examples from dipinti are: **sella**, 'seat,' acc. sg. fem.; **equa**, 'mare,' acc. sg. fem.; **Deciu**, gentilicium, acc. sg. masc.; etc. Examples from graffiti are: **Fortunatu**, cognomen, acc. sg. masc.; **plurima**, 'very big,' acc. sg. fem.; **pane**, 'bread,' acc. sg. fem., etc. Interestingly, a few examples of hypercorrect spellings in which an **m** was erroneously added to an ablative case form exist, e.g., **permissūm**, 'permission,' abl. sg. masc.; **diēm**, 'day,' abl. sg. masc. These spellings support the idea that the vowel of the accusative singular was lengthened in compensation for loss of final **m**.

s: Word-final **s** was rarely omitted in Pompeiian wall inscriptions. A few examples are attested after the short vowels **u** and **o**, and there is an example after short **i**. Loss of **s** after long vowels is even rarer, there being but a half dozen examples altogether after **ā**, **ē** and **ō**. Examples are: **Aemiliu**, gentilicium, nom. sg. masc.; **servo**, 'servant,' nom. sg. masc.; **Romulu**, cognomen, nom. sg. masc.; **Purami**, cognomen, nom. sg. fem., cf. **Pyramis**; **fēlīcitā**, 'happiness,' nom. sg. fem., cf. **fēlīcitās**; **Decembrē**, 'December,' acc. pl. fem.

t: In monosyllables there was confusion between **t** and **d**. So, for example, the preposition **ad** was also spelled **at** and the conjunction **at** was spelled **ad**. This confusion arose because final **t** and **d** in words like **ad**, **at**, etc., were assimilated in voicing to the initial sound of the following word. Note also **set** for **sed**, and **quit** for **quid**.

In the speech of some Pompeiians, word-final **t** in polysyllabic words, especially third singular active verb forms, was weakly articulated. This was reflected in two ways: (1) by spelling original final **t** by **d**, as in the third singular verb form **rogad**, 'requests,' 3rd sg. pres. act., cf. **rogat**; and (2) by omission of final **t** altogether, as in **face**, 'makes,' 3rd sg. pres., cf. **facit**. Examples of **t** spelled by **d** are: **diced**, 'says,' 3rd sg. pres. act.; **inquid**, 'says,' 3rd sg. pres. act.; **rogad**, 'requests,' 3rd sg. pres. act. Examples of loss of word-final **t** are: **ama**, 'loves,' 3rd sg. pres. act.; cf. **amat**; **valia**, 'fare well,' 3rd sg. pres. subj. act.; cf. **valeat**; **peria**, 'perish', 3rd sg. pres. subj. act.; cf. **pereat**; **nōsci** (= **nōn sci**), 'not know', 3rd sg. pres. act.; cf. **nescit**.

§2.2 Declension

First Declension Genitive Singular

There are several examples of the first declension genitive singular ending **-aes**. The final **-s** of this ending may be due to the influence of Greek first declension feminines ending in -ης or -ας, but this is not certain. Examples are: **Cominiaes**, cognomen, gen. sg. fem.; **Liviaes**, gentilicium, gen. sg. fem.; **cōpōniaes**, 'belonging to an inn or tavern,' gen. sg. fem.; etc.

First Declension Dative Singular

The dative singular ending of first declension nouns and adjectives was **-ae**. However, the ending **-ē**, which comes from **-ae** by monophthongization (§2.1), is attested frequently in graffiti, and may actually be more frequent than the spelling system permits us to know. Examples are: **suē**, 'her own,' dat. sg. fem., cf. **suae**; **Prīmē**, cognomen, dat. sg. fem., cf. **Prīmae**.

Second Declension Vocative Singular

The regular vocative singular ending for second declension nouns of the **-ius** class was long **ī**, and this is the form that appears in wall inscriptions. Examples of vocative singulars of this type are: **Clōdī**, gentilicium, voc. sg. masc.; **Seī**, gentilicium, voc. sg. masc.; **Obellī**, gentilicium, voc. sg. masc.; **Trebī**, gentilicium, voc. sg. masc.; **lanternārī**, 'lantern bearer,' voc. sg. masc.; **lanifricārī**, 'wool-worker,' voc. sg. masc.

Second Declension Genitive Singular

The regular genitive singular ending for second declension nouns of the **-ius** class was long **-ī**. This ending was NOT a contraction of

iī, but a replacement of the original stem forming suffix **-io** by a long **-ī**. At Pompeii and Herculaneum, then, genitive singular forms such as **Suedī**, **Nigidī**, **Suettī**, and **fīlī** attest the regular genitive singular ending. The ending **-iī** is found in very few wall inscriptions, e.g., **Numisiī**, gen. sg. masc. (see III, 2, 8).

Second Declension Nominative/Vocative Plural

The nominative/vocative plural of second declension nouns of the **-ius** class regularly ended in long **-ī**, an ending which was the result of contraction of the stem vowel **-i** and the plural ending **-ī**. Thus original **-iī** contracted to **-ī**. Examples are legion: **pomārī**, 'fruit-vendors,' nom. pl. masc., cf. **pomāriī**; **pomārī**, voc. pl. masc., cf. **pomāriī**.

First and Second Declension Dative/Ablative Plural

For noun and adjective forms ending in **-ia** (first declension) and **-ius**, **-ium** (second declension) the dative/ablative plural ending **-īs** regularly contracted with the stem-final vowel **-i**, yielding **-īs**. Examples are: **latrunculārīs**, 'player in a board game,' abl. pl. masc., cf. **latruculāriīs**; **praedīs**, 'property,' abl. pl. neut., cf. **praediīs**; etc. Examples of uncontracted **-iīs** are rare, there being only a few examples attested in the entire corpus of wall inscriptions, e.g., **iudiciīs**, 'decisions,' dat. pl. neut. See §2.1 Contraction.

Consonant-Stem Genitive Singular

The consonant-stem genitive singular ending **-us** is found in a couple of words, e.g., **aerus**, 'money,' gen. sg. neut., cf. **aeris**. Interestingly, this ending is attested sporadically in Republican Latin inscriptions from as early as the third century BC, and so must have survived as a regional variant of the regular genitive singular ending **-is**.

§2.3 Conjugation

Second Singular Deponent/Passive

There are two, possibly three, forms that show a second singular deponent/passive ending with the form **-rus**, rather than expected -

ris or **-re**. The ending **-rus** is found also in several dialectal Latin inscriptions from the late Republican period and so, like the consonant-stem genitive singular **-us**, the second singular verb ending **-rus** appears to have survived as a regional variant of **-ris** and **-re**. Examples are: **fīgārus**, 'may you be fastened,' 2nd sg. pres. pass. subj., cf. **fīgāris**; **frūniscārus**, 'may you enjoy,' 2nd sg. pres. depon. subj., cf. **frūniscāris**; and possibly **[oblivīscār]us**, 'may you forget,' 2nd sg. pres. dep. subj.

Deponents

The general trend in Vulgar Latin was to eliminate deponent formations in favor of active ones. Several verbs that were deponent in literary Latin were active at Pompeii, e.g., **abominō**, 'I despise,' 1st sg. pres. act., cf. **abominor**; **luctābās**, 'you wrestled,' 2nd sg. impf. act., cf. **luctābāris**; **rixsātis**, 'you all brawl,' 2nd pl. pres. act., cf. **rixāminī**; **testificō**, 'I testify to,' 1st sg. pres. act., cf. **testificor**; **tūtat,** 'he protects,' 3rd sg. pres. act., cf. **tūtātur**.

Perfect Tense

For first conjugation forms, so-called 'syncopated' or 'contracted' perfects were the rule for the first and third plural and the second singular and second plural. Examples are: **commodāstī**, 'you provided,' 2nd sg. perf. act., cf. **commodāvistī**; **probāstis,** 'you all approved,' 2nd pl. perf. act., cf. **probāvistis**; **habitārunt**, 'they lived,' 3rd pl. perf. act., cf. **habitāvērunt**; **cēnāsse**, 'to eat,' inf. perf. act., cf. **cēnāvisse**.

So-called 'syncopated' forms were found also for second and third conjugation verbs, e.g., **explēstei**, 'you accomplished,' 2nd sg. perf. act., cf. **explēvistī**; **dēdūcxstis**, 'you all extended,' 2nd pl. perf. act., cf. **dēdūxistis**; **nōstei**, 'you know,' 2nd sg. perf. act., cf. **nōvistī**. For fourth conjugation verbs, and for the verb **eō**, 'go,' intervocalic **v** was lost and the two **i**-vowels contracted, as in **fastidī**, 'I scorned,' 1st sg. perf. act., cf. **fastidiī**, **fastidīvī**; **pereit** (**ei** spells long **ī** here), 'he died,' 3rd sg. perf. act., cf. **periit**.

§2.4 Syntax

Accusative in lists, etc.

In accounts, lists, and inventories of foodstuffs, household objects, etc., nouns were inflected for accusative case without any verb being expressed (see inscription (19) cited above). It is possible to understand a verb of buying and/or selling for some inscriptions, but for other inscriptions in which objects were listed as part of an inventory a verb of buying/selling is not apropos. It appears that the accusative case has come to be seen as the standard case for listing items to be purchased or sold, or for making an inventory of household items, etc.

Ablative for Locative

For first and second declension nouns, the ablative without a preposition was often used with locative function, so, for example, **Nolā**, 'at Nola,' abl. sg. fem., **Herclāniō**, 'at Herculaneum,' abl. sg. neut., and **Nucereā**, 'at Nuceria,' abl. sg. fem. Compare the locatives **Romae**, 'at Rome,' loc. sg. fem., **Herculānī**, 'at Herculaneum,' loc. sg. neut., and **Nuceriae**, 'at Nuceria,' loc. sg. fem.

Prepositions

The prepositions **ā/ab**, **cum**, and **prō** were occasionally used with the accusative case rather than the ablative case, which is the classical Latin norm. Examples are: **cum sodālēs**, 'with colleagues'; **cum discentēs**, 'with apprentices'; **prō ferrum**, 'instead of iron'; **ā pulvīnar**, 'from the *pulvinar*.'

The preposition **in**, when governing the accusative case, expressed the idea of movement towards a goal. At Pompeii, however, this notion was expressed also by **in** followed by the ablative case, as in **in conventū vēnī**, 'I came to the meeting.'

§2.5 Punctuation

Punctuation was a common feature of dipinti and graffiti. In many inscriptions, particularly dipinti, words were separated from one another by interpuncts placed at mid-line level, e.g., **C · I ·**

Polybium, inscription (1) above (see also Facsimile 1). Interpuncts were used consistently in electoral announcements, gladiatorial announcements, and other inscriptions of a more public nature. Interpuncts were also common in graffiti (see Facsimile 10), though not as common as in dipinti. Other forms of punctuation to separate words were rare. Several graffiti, e.g., II, 2, 42 and II, 2, 43, had dashes separating words rather than interpuncts. In one dipinto, viz., II, 7, 97, words were separated by means of tiny leaves.

In general there was no punctuation separating sentences, though there is one graffito in which the dash appears to be used to mark off one sentence from another. If this is the function of the dash in this inscription, it is, as far as I am aware, the only example of sentential punctuation in the Pompeian corpus.

Some graffiti did not employ any form of punctuation, but separated words from one another by means of spacing, similar to the convention employed in the writing of English. In other graffiti, all of the words were written together without any breaks, so called *scriptio continua* (see Facsimile 11).

§2.6 Synopsis of Features of Orthography and Language

Orthography and Phonology

1. Long Vowels: **ei** spells ī, e.g., **Eidūs** (cf. **Īdūs**)
2. Contraction: contraction of **iī** to **ī**, e.g., **iudicīs** (cf. **iudiciīs**)
3. Monophthongization: monophthongization of **ae** to **ē**, e.g., **Prīmē** (cf. **Prīmae**)
4. Short **i** and **u** in Medial Syllables: fluctuation in spelling of short high vowel before labial consonants in open medial syllables, e.g., **optumē** vs. **optimōs**
5. Short **i** in Final Syllables: short **i** is changed to short **e** in word-final syllables, e.g., **dīcet** (cf. **dīcit**)
6. Hiatus: short **e** is changed to **i** before another vowel, e.g., **habiās** (cf. **habeās**)
7. Syncope: short vowels are lost in open medial syllables, e.g., **domnus** (cf. **dominus**)
8. **h**: loss of initial **h**, e.g., **abiās** (cf. **habeās**)

9. **b** and **v**: pronunciation of word-initial **v** as [β], e.g., **benī** (cf. **venī**); pronunciation of intervocalic **b** as [β], e.g., **tivi** (cf. **tibi**)
10. Nasal + Stop Consonant: loss of nasal before stop consonant, e.g., **vedes** (cf. **vendis**)
11. **ns**: loss of **n** before **s**, e.g., **Crēscēs** (cf. **Crēscēns**)
12. Word-final Consonants. loss of word-final **m**, **s**, and **t**, e.g., **Venere**, **Deciu**, etc. (cf. **Venerem**, **Decium**)

Declension

1. First Declension Genitive Singular, e.g., **Liviaes** (cf. **Liviae**)
2. First Declension Dative Singular, e.g., **suē** (cf. **suae**)
3. Second Declension Vocative Singular, e.g., **Clōdī**
4. Second Declension Genitive Singular, e.g., **fīlī**
5. Second Declension Nominative/Vocative Plural, e.g., **plōstrārī** (cf. **plaustrāriī**)
6. First and Second Declension Dative/Ablative Plural, e.g., **iūdicīs** (cf. **iūdiciīs**)
7. Third Declension Genitive Singular, e.g., **aerus** (cf. **aeris**)

Conjugation

1. Second Singular Deponent/Passive, e.g., **fīgārus** (cf. **fīgāris**)
2. Perfect Tense, e.g., **commodāstī** (cf. **commodāvistī**)
3. Deponents, e.g., **rixsātis** (cf. **rixāminī**)

Syntax

1. Accusative in accounts and lists
2. Ablative for Locative, e.g., **Herclāniō** (cf. **Herculānī**)
3. Prepositions, e.g., **cum discentēs**

Punctuation

1. Interpuncts, e.g., **C · I · Polybium**

§3. Features of the Text

§3.1 Organization

The inscriptions are organized into three units. Unit I is dipinti (painted inscriptions) from Pompeii: electoral announcements (*programmata*), advertisements for gladiatorial games (*edicta munerum*), and other types of inscriptions. Unit II is graffiti from Pompeii and from a few *villae rusticae* located close to the city. The graffiti are organized into subsections based on topic or theme, e.g., graffiti pertaining to soldiers, graffiti with amatory themes, etc. The inscriptions from Herculaneum, both dipinti and graffiti, are lumped together into a single, short unit (Unit III).

§3.2 Entries for Inscriptions

The inscriptions in this text were collected from Vol. IV of the *Corpus Inscriptionum Latinarum (CIL).* A few inscriptions, yet to appear in *CIL*, were taken from articles by Giordano (1966), Giordano and Casale (1990), Pagano (1987), Solin (1975), and Varone (1987) (for complete references, see §4. Bibliography: Articles on Inscriptions).

The inscriptions in this book are numbered serially within each unit. Thus, the first inscription of Unit I (**Dipinti**), Section 1 (**1. Electoral Announcements**) has the reference number I, 1, 1 = Unit 1, Section 1, Inscription 1.

The entry for each inscription is divided into three fields of information: (i) header, (ii) text of the inscription, (iii) grammatical notes and commentary (see infra, §3.3).

The header includes several distinct pieces of information. There are two reference numbers. The first number is the reference number of the inscription in this text. The second number is the one assigned to the inscription in *CIL*. Next comes the location in Pompeii or Herculaneum where the inscription was found. For Pompeii this information is presented in the following order: region of the city (Roman capitals), *insula* number (small Roman numerals), and entranceway (Arabic numerals). For most inscriptions from Herculaneum the find-spot is indicated by *insula* number (small Roman numerals) and entranceway (Arabic numerals). Graffiti from *villae rusticae* are indicated by the location of the villa, e.g., Boscoreale. The final section of the entry is the name of the street on which the inscription was found, e.g., Via Stabiana. For inscriptions in which it was impossible to determine the location, I employ question marks in place of region, *insula*, and entranceway numbers, e.g., V, ?, ?; Via di Nola.

The second field of information is the inscription itself. I employ many of the standard conventions for the presentation of Latin inscriptions, but I have also adopted several idiosyncratic features (for which, see §3.4).

Following the text of the inscription are notes and commentary. In this section I discuss unusual features of the inscriptions, such as uncommon abbreviations, peculiarities of orthography and language, and other information that is deemed to be relevant and useful for interpretation. Words appearing in the notes or commentary are cross-referenced to the line of text in which they appear by means of a superscript number. Thus, the superscript [2] prefixed to the word **cōpō**, i.e., [2]**cōpō**, indicates that this word is found in line 2 of the text.

§3.3 Sample Inscription

A sample entry for a dipinto, an electoral announcement, is given in (24). The information contained in the headers is described above in section §3.2. The inscription is found in Unit I, Section 1, which is the section on electoral announcements.

(24) Entry for painted wall inscription:

34. 3502; VI, xiv, 39; Vicolo dei Vetti.

[Holc]onium · Priscum aed · Clodi · fac ·
Sei · copo · probe · fecisti
quod · sella · commodasti

[1]**Clōdī**: voc. sg. masc. [2]**Sēī**: voc. sg. masc. of **Sēius**. [2]**cōpō**: voc. sg. masc.; cf. **caupō**. §2.1 Monophthongization. [3]**sella**: §2.1 Word-final Consonants: **m**. [3]**commodāstī**: 2nd sg. perf. act. §2.3 Perfect Tense Forms. The inscription is divided into two syntactic units. The first sentence is line 1. Lines 2 and 3 form the second sentence. The meaning of the **quod**-clause is not entirely clear. Some scholars think that **Sēius**, the inn-keeper, provided the painter with a chair or stool so that he could rest after painting (the announcement is located too high on the wall for the scriptor to have painted while he was seated).

This inscription has a key number of I, 1, 34, which indicates that it is the thirty-fourth text in Unit I, Section 1. The *CIL* number is Vol. IV.3502. The inscription was painted on the wall of *Domus* 39, which was located in *Regio* VI, *Insula* xiv, on the street named *Vicolo dei Vetti*. The notes following the inscription provide information about linguistic features characteristic of wall inscriptions at Pompeii. Particularly noteworthy features are the monophthongization of **au**, e.g., **caupō** vs. **cōpō**, the omission of word-final **-m**, and the so-called 'syncopated' form of the first conjugation perfect, a form that was common at Pompeii. These features are discussed in greater detail at §2.1 Monophthongization, §2.1 Word-final Consonants: **m**, and §2.3 Perfect Tense Forms, respectively.

§3.4 Conventions in Inscriptions

All inscriptions, whether painted or incised with stylus, are printed in boldface type. For the most part, standard epigraphical conventions are employed in the presentation of texts. Curly brackets { x } indicate extra characters introduced by scribal error. Angled brackets < x > indicate characters omitted by scribal error, but added to the text by the editor. Letters incorrectly incised or painted, which are corrected by the editor, are also placed within angled brackets. Word dividers are indicated by a period · set at mid-line level. When other forms of punctuation are used, these are indicated by diacritics that correspond in reasonably close fashion to the form of puncutation, e.g., – for a dash. Characters that have been 'erased,' by whatever means, but can still be read, are indicated by double square brackets **[[** x **]]**. Characters that are no longer legible and have been restored by modern editors are placed within single square brackets **[** x **]**. In cases where it is impossible to restore portions of the text, dots within square brackets **[. . .]** are used to indicate the number of missing characters. Where the amount of text that has been lost cannot be determined, three dashes are placed within square brackets, thus **[– – –]**.

I have departed from standard epigraphical practice in several respects. First of all, I do not indicate combinations of letters written by means of ligatures. Also, I do not indicate apices over vowels or the special forms of the letter **i** known as I-*longa* (for discussion see §2.1 Long vowels). The letter **u** is represented in the text by the characters **u** and **v**, according to the standard method of transcription. Contrary to the customary practice, I do not fill in abbreviations in the text (see §3.5 below). Common abbreviations are listed in an appendix (Abbreviations in Wall Inscriptions) in the rear of the book. Finally, I do not indicate characters whose reading is uncertain, a feature that would be indicated according to standard epigraphical practice by use of the underdot. Instead, these characters are treated as being illegible and so are placed within single square brackets **[x]**.

Vowel length is not indicated on words in inscriptions, but it is marked on all words discussed in the notes. Vowel length is also marked for all words in the list of abbreviations, in the index, and in the vocabulary.

Proper names are capitalized, as are the names of months and the names of the parts of Roman months. In order to distinguish numbers from letters, numbers are printed in capitals.

Many of the inscriptions in this book are written *scriptio continua*, without any word-breaks, e.g., **nihildurare**. I have printed these inscriptions with the appropiate divisions into words, e.g., **nihil durare**.

I have not attempted to reproduce the exact disposition and layout of dipinti or graffiti, but I have tried to follow, inasmuch as it was possible, the division of the texts into lines. In cases where one line of an inscription was too long to fit the space available in this book, I have placed the run-over on the following line with indentation, thus indicating that the indented line is to be read as part of the line directly above it.

§3.5 Noteworthy Features

Two features of this text require special comment. As noted earlier, one of the pervasive features of *programmata* and *edicta munerum* is the great number of abbreviations. Abbreviations such as **o · v · f** or **ovf** (**ōrō vōs faciātis**) are so common that they can easily be committed to memory. For common abbreviations, then, the first occurrence is flagged in the notes but subsequent occurrences are not, and so the reader must be prepared to memorize the abbreviations or refer to the list of abbreviations located at the end of the text. Idiosyncratic abbreviations are discussed in the notes appended to the inscription in question.

The language of wall inscriptions from Pompeii and Herculaneum exhibits many features of orthography and language that are not attested, or are infrequently attested, in the literary language. Features that occur repeatedly in the inscriptions are discussed in sections §2.1 through §2.5 of the Introduction (a Synopsis of Features of Orthography and Grammar appears in section §2.6), and it is assumed that the reader will become familiar with them. When these features are found in inscriptions for the first time, they are noted and discussed in the commentary, but subsequent occurrences are indicated only by reference to the appropriate sections of the Introduction.

§3.6 Phonetic Alphabet

In a few cases it has been necessary to use the phonetic alphabet to describe the sounds that certain letters or combinations of letters represented. For example, the digraph **ae** occasionally represented a simple vowel with the sound value of [ɛ] as, for example, in the name **Graphicae**, voc. sg. masc. of **Graphicus**. This sound was roughly the one found in Modern English *bed*. A list of the letters of the phonetic alphabet used in this text along with words containing equivalents of these sounds is given in (25).

(25) Letters of the Phonetic Alphabet

Phonetic alphabet	approximate
vowel [ɪ]	English vowel in *bid*
vowel [ɛ]	English vowel in *bed*
vowel [ɛ:]	English vowel in *bed*, but long
vowel [ɔ]	Dialectal English vowel in *caught*
diphthong [ay]	English diphthong in *buy*

consonant [β]	Spanish consonant **b** in *saber,* 'to know'
consonant [w]	English consonant **w** in *we*
consonant [r]	Italian consonant **r** in *roba,* 'stuff'
consonant [l]	English consonant **l** in *leaf*
consonant [t]	English consonant **t** in *pat*
consonant [k]	English consonant **k** in *make*

§4. Bibliography

The Bibliography is divided into five sections. Section One is the *Corpus Inscriptionum Latinarum,* Vol. IV. This is the scholarly edition of all Pompeiian inscriptions, including wall inscriptions, inscriptions engraved on stone, and inscriptions incised on ceramic and on other materials. Section Two is a short list of books that contain selections of wall inscriptions. Some of the books, such as Antonio Varrone's *Erotica Pompeiiana,* are organized around particular themes. Others, such as Diehl's *Pompeianische Wandinschriften,* aim at a representative selection of the material. Section Three is a very short list of articles on Pompeiian inscriptions. These articles, which contain references to other important papers, may serve as a springboard for further investigation. Section Four is a selection of books about Pompeiian material culture, politics, etc. Again, this is a subject with extensive literature, but most of the books in this section have substantial bibliographical references. The topic of the final section is Vulgar Latin. Of particular importance here is Veikko Väänänen's *Le latin vulgaire des inscriptions pompeiennes,* which is a comprehensive description of the linguistic features of the wall inscriptions.

Corpus Inscriptionum Latinarum

Zangemeister, Carolus. 1871. *Corpus Inscriptionum Latinarum IV. Inscriptiones parietariae Pompeianae Herculanenses Stabianae.* Berlin: Georg Reimer.

———. 1898. *Corpus Inscriptionum Latinarum IV.* Supplementum, pars prior: *Tabulae ceratae Pompeis repertae annis MDCCCLXXV et MDCCCLXXXVII.* Berlin: Georg Reimer.

Mau, Augustus et Carolus Zangemeister. 1909. *Corpus Inscriptionum Latinarum IV. Supplementum, pars posterior: Inscriptiones parietariae et uasorum fictilium.* Berlin: Georg Reimer.

Delle Corte, Matthaeo. 1952. *Corpus Inscriptionum Latinarum IV. Supplementi pars tertia. Inscriptiones Pompeianae parietariae et uasorum fictilium.* Berlin: Georg Reimer.

———. 1955. *Corpus Inscriptionum Latinarum IV. Supplementi tertii: Inscriptiones Pompeianae parietariae et uasorum fictilium.* Berlin: De Gruyter.

———. 1963. *Corpus Inscriptionum Latinarum IV. Inscriptiones Pompeianae parietariae et uasorum fictilium. Supplementi tertii pars tertia.* Berlin: De Gruyter.

Weber, F. et Pius Ciprotti. 1970. *Corpus Inscriptionum Latinarum IV. Supplementi tertii pars tertia 4: Inscriptiones parietariae et uasorum fictilium annis 1951–1956 repertae. Inscriptiones Herculanenses parietariae et vasorum fictilium.* Berlin: De Gruyter.

Collections of Inscriptions

Canali, Luca, & Guglielmo Cavallo. 1991. *Graffiti latini : scrivere sui muri a Roma antica.* Milano: Bompiani.

Diehl, Ernst. 1930. *Pompeianische Wandinschriften und Verwandtes,* 2nd ed. Bonn: A. Marcus & E. Weber.

Geist, Hieronymus. 1960. *Pompeianische Wandinschriften. 400 Originaltexte mit Übersetzung und Angabe des Fundortes.* 2. erweiterte Aufl. unter Mitwirkung von Werner Krenkel. München: Ernst Heimeran.

Krenkel, Werner. 1963. *Pompejanische Inschriften.* Leipzig.

Sabbatini Tumolesi, Patrizia. 1980. *Gladiatorum paria. Annunci di spettacoli gladiatori a Pompei.* Roma.

Staccioli, R. A. 1992. *Manifesti elettorali nell'antica Pompei.* Milano.

Väänänen, Veikko. 1962. *Graffiti di Pompei e di Roma.* Roma: Amici di Villa Lante al Gianicolo.

Varone, Antonio. 1994. *Erotica pompeiana: iscrizioni d'amore sui muri di Pompei.* Roma: L'Erma di Bretschneider.

Weeber Karl-Wilhelm. 1996. *Decius war hier— : das Beste aus der römischen Graffiti-Szene.* Zurich: Artemis & Winkler.

Wick, F. C. 1926. *Inscrizioni metriche pompeiane*. Milano: Albrighi & Segati.

Articles on Inscriptions

Ciprotti, Pio. 1967. Die Graffiti. *Altertum* 13.85–94.

Della Corte, Matteo. 1958. Le iscrizioni di Ercolano. *Rendiconti dell' Accademia di Archeologia, Lettere e Belle Arti di Napoli* 33.239-308.

Giordano, Carlo. 1966. Le iscrizioni della casa di M. Fabio Rufo. *Rendiconti dell' Accademia di Archeologia Lettere e Belle Arti di Napoli* 41.73–89.

Giordano, Carlo & Angelandrea Casale. 1990. Iscrizioni pompeiane inedite scoperte tra gli anni 1954–1978. *Atti della Accademia Pontaniana* 39.273–378.

Pagano, Mario. 1987. Una iscrizione elettorale da Ercolano. *Cronache Ercolanesi* 17.151-152.

Solin, Heikki. 1973. Review of *CIL IV, Suppl. 3, 3–4,* in *Gnomon* 45.258-277.

———. 1975. Die Wandinschriften in sog. Haus des M. Fabius Rufus. *Neue Forschungen in Pompeji und den anderen vom Vesuvausbruch 79 n. Chr. verschūtten Stādten* hrsg. von B. Andreae und H. Kyrieleis, 243–266. Recklinghausen.

———. 1979. Le iscrizioni parietali. *Pompei '79. Raccolta di studi per il decimonono centenario dell'eruzione vesuviana* a cura di F. Zevi, 278-288. Napoli.

Varone, Antonio. 1987. Nuovi tituli picti pompeiani. *Rivista di studi pompeiani* 1.91–106.

Pompeii

Castrén, P. 1975. *Ordo populusque Pompeianus. Polity and Society in Roman Pompeii.* Roma.

Etienne, Robert. 1998 (5th ed.). *La Vie quotidienne à Pompéi.* Paris: Hachette.

Franklin, James L. 1980. *Pompeii : the electoral programmata, campaigns, and politics, A.D. 71-79.* Rome: American Academy in Rome.

———. 1999. *Pompeis difficile est: studies in the political life of imperial Pompeii.* Ann Arbor: University of Michigan Press.

Mau, Augustus [translated by Francis W. Kelsey]. 1902. *Pompeii. Its Life and Art.* New York: The Macmillan Co.
Moeller, W. O. 1970. The riot of A.D. 59 at Pompeii. *Historia* 19.84–96.
Mouritsen, Henrik. 1988. *Elections, magistrates, and municipal elite: studies in Pompeian epigraphy.* Roma: "L'Erma" di Bretschneider.
Tanzer, Helen Henrietta. 1939. *The common people of Pompeii; a study of the graffiti.* Baltimore: The Johns Hopkins Press.
Willems, Pierre Gaspard Hubert. 1969. *Les elections municipales a Pompeii.* Amsterdam: Rodopi.
Zanker, Paul [translated by Deborah Lucas Schneider]. 1998. *Pompeii: public and private life.* Cambridge, Mass.: Harvard University Press.

Vulgar Latin

Herman, Jozsef [translated by Roger Wright]. 2000. *Vulgar Latin.* University Park, PA: Pennsylvania State University.
Palmer, Leonard R. 1954. Vulgar Latin. *The Latin Language,* pp. 148–180. London: Faber & Faber.
Pisani, Vittore. 1950. *Testi latini arcaici e volgari con commento glottologico.* Torino: Rosenberg and Sellier.
Väänänen, Veikko. 1966. *Le latin vulgaire des inscriptions pompeiennes.* 3e ed. augm. Berlin: Akademie-Verlag.
———. 1981. *Introduction au Latin Vulgaire. 3rd edition.* Paris: Klincksieck.

An Introduction to WALL INSCRIPTIONS from Pompeii and Herculaneum

I. DIPINTI FROM POMPEII

1. Electoral Announcements

1. 61; VIII, iii or iv, ?; Via dei Teatri.

M · Marium
aed · faci
oro · vos

[Facsimile 10] This dipinto is among the oldest at Pompeii. It can be dated to the end of the Republic, circa 80–30 BC. [1]**M**: abbrev. for **Mārcum**, praenomen, acc. sg. masc. [2]**aed**: abbrev. for **aedīlem**. [2]**faci**: abbrev. for **faciātis**.

2. 103; VI, i, 17–18; Via Consolare.

M · Holconium · Priscum
G · Gavium · Rufum · II · vir
Phoebus · cum · emptoribus
suis · rogat

Priscus and Rufus were candidates for AD 79, the year the city was destroyed. [2]**G**: abbrev. for **Gāium**, praenomen, acc. sg. masc. [2]**II · vir**: abbrev. for **duovirōs** or **duumvirōs**. [3]**Phoebus**: cognomen of Greek origin. [3]**ēmptōribus**: this word can mean 'buyer, purchaser, customer.'

3. 120; VII, ins. occ., 10–20; Via Consolare.

M · Cerrinium · Vatiam ·
aed · o · v · fac ·
Fabius · Eupor · rog
et scr Infan[ti]o

Vatia's candidacy probably dates to the last ten years of the city. [2]**ō · v · fac**: abbrev. for **ōrō vōs faciātis**. [3]**Eupor**: cognomen of Greek origin. [3]**rog**: abbrev. for **rogat**. [4]**scr**: abbrev. for **scrībit**. [4]**Īnfan[ti]ō**: name of the sign painter. This inscription has three syntactic units: (1) lines 1–2; (2) line 3; (3) line 4.

4. 128; VI, ins. occ., 10–20; Via Consolare.

M · Cerrinium
aed · Salinienses
rog ·

For the date of the candidacy, see I, 1, 3. [2]**Saliniēnsēs**: inhabitants of a Pompeian neighborhood located near the **Porta Salis**, which is today known as the Porta Ercolano. [3]**rog**: abbrev. for **rogant**.

5. 149; VI, ix, 6–7; Via di Mercurio.

M · Cerrinium
aed · pomari · rog

For the date of the candidacy, see I, 1, 3. [2]**pomārī**: nom. pl. masc. See §2.1 Contraction and §2.2 2nd Declension Nominative/Vocative Plural. The suffix **-ārius** is used to form nouns indicating occupations. There are many such formations found in the wall inscriptions.

6. 171; VI, ix, 6–7; Via di Mercurio.

A · Vettium Firmum
aed · o · v · f · dign · est
Caprasia · cum · Nymphio · rog
una · et · vicini · o v f

The candidacy of Aulus Vettius Firmus belongs to the first half of the 70s AD. [1]**A**: abbrev. for **Aulum**. [2]**ō · v · f**: abbrev. for **ōrō vōs faciātis**. [3]**Caprāsia**: note that the supporter is a female. This is interesting because women could not vote in Pompeiian elections. We may suppose that Caprasia and her husband (?), Nymphius, were proprietors of an inn. [3]**rog**: the subject of this verb is **Caprāsia**. [4]**ūnā**: probably to be taken with the preposition **cum**, 'together with.' [4]**vīcīnī**: voc. pl. masc. [4]**ō v f**: understand a pronominal form referring to the candidate **Aulus Vettius Firmus**. Divide into four syntactic units: (1) lines 1–2, **A** to **f**; (2) line 2, **dign · est**; (3) lines 3–4, **Caprāsia** to **ūnā**; (4) line 4, **et vīcīnī ō v f**.

7. 174; VI, ix, 11–12; Via di Mercurio.

A · Vettium · Firmum
aed · v · b · o · v · f · Felix · cupit

For the date of the candidacy, see I, 1, 6. [2]**v · b**: abbrev. for **virum bonum**. [2]**Fēlīx**: begin a new sentence with this word. [2]**cupit**: understand as direct object a pronoun referring to the election of **Aulus Vettius Firmus**.

8. 183; VI, viii, 12–13; Via di Mercurio.

Vettium
Firmum
aed o · v · f · dign
est · pomari · facite

For the date of the candidacy, see I, 1, 6. [2]**dign**: abbrev. for **dignus**. [4]**pomārī**: voc. pl. masc. §2.1 Contraction and §2.2 2nd Declension Nominative/Vocative Plural. [4]**facite**: understand as direct object **Aulum Vettium Firmum aedīlem**.

9. 187; VI, viii, 13–14; Via di Mercurio.

L · Veranium · Hypsaeum
II · vir · i · d · tertio · quinq
Casellium · Marcellum
aed · optimos · collegas

This announcement supports the candidacies of two men. The dating is uncertain, although AD 75 is possible. [1]**L**: abbrev. for **Lūcium**. [2]**II· vir · i · d**: abbrev. for **duumvirum iūrē dīcendō**. [2]**tertiō**: adv., 'for the third time.' [2]**quinq**: abbrev. for **quinquennālem**. The title **duumvirī quinquennālēs** was borne by the duumvirs at Pompeii every fifth year, during which time they had additional powers, including revising the rolls of the census. [4]**optimōs collēgās**: in apposition to the names of the two candidates. Supply the verb phrase **ō v f** and take the names of both candidates as direct objects.

10. 221; VI, viii, 20; Via di Mercurio.

M · Cerrinium · Vatiam

2 **aed · dignum rei · p · Tyrranus · cupiens**
3 **fecit · cum · sodales**

For the date of the candidacy, see I, 1, 3. [2]**dignum**: in electoral announcements this word regularly governs the genitive case. See I, 1, 42 for **dignum** governing the ablative. [2]**p**: abbrev. for **pūblicae.** [2]**Tyrranus**: cognomen of Greek origin. The supporter is a Greek freedman. **cupiens**: the adjective governs the accusatives. [3]**fēcit**: refers to the painting of the electoral announcement. [3]**cum sodālēs**: the preposition **cum** governs the accusative case. §2.4 Prepositions.

11. 222; VI, viii, 20; Via di Mercurio.

1 **P · Paquium · Proculum · II · vir virum b · d · r · [p]**
2 **ovf**
3 **A · Vettium [· Caprasi]um · Felicem · II · vir · v · b · d · r · p · ovf digni sunt**
4 **Q · Marium [Rufum] M · Epidium · Sabinum · aediles · v · a · s · p · p · ovf · digni · sunt**
5 **s[cri]bit · [Os]sius · de · albatore · Onesimo**

This electoral announcement is of particular interest because it mentions the names of four candidates, two standing for the duumvirate, and two standing for the office of aedile. The candidates stood for office in the first half of the 70s AD. [1]**P**: abbrev. for **Pūblium.** [1]**b**: abbrev. for **bonum.** [1]**d · r · [p]**: abbrev. for **dignum reī pūblicae.** [4]**Q**: abbrev. for **Quīntum.** [4]**v · a · s · p · p**: abbrev. for **viīs aedīlibus sacrīs pūblicīsque prōcūrandīs.** [5]**dē · albātōre**: note that the prefix **dē-** is separated by a word punct from its noun **albātōre**. There are several examples in Pompeiian wall inscriptions where the constituents of words are separated by word puncts, e.g., I, 1, 22. **Dēalbātor** refers to the fellow who whitewashed the walls before the electoral announcements were painted on them. This announcement has three major sections: (1) lines 1–3; (2) line 4; and (3) line 5.

12. 275; VII, iv, 62–63; Via della Fortuna.

1 **C · Cuspium · Pansam**
2 **aed · d · r · [p] ovf · Saturninus**
3 **cum · discentes · rog**

Pānsa stood for the office of aedile in AD 79. [1]**C**: abbrev. for **Gāium**. [2]**Saturnīnus**: begin a new sentence here. [3]**cum discentēs**: §2.4 Prepositions. [3]**discentēs**: refers here to 'apprentices.' [3]**rog**: as direct object understand **Pānsam**.

13. 336; VI, xiv, 12 or 15; Via della Fortuna.

Sallustium · Capitonem · aed
o · v · f · caupones · facite

The date of this candidacy is unknown. [2]**caupōnēs**: voc. pl. masc. [2]**facite**: as direct object understand the name of the candidate and the office.

14. 357; IX, v, 11; Via di Nola.

Helvium · Sabinum
Poppaei · aed · fieri rog

The candidacy dates to AD 79. [2]**Poppaeī**: nom. pl. masc., 'members of Poppaea family.' **Poppaea Sabīna**, who belonged to an influential Pompeiian family, became wife of the emperor Nero in AD 62. She died in AD 64. [2]**aed**: predicate noun after **fierī**.

15. 423; IX, ?, ?; Via di Nola.

C · Calventium
Sittium · II · v · i · d ·
ego
Astylus · sum

Sittius probably stood for the duumvirate in the second half of the 70s AD. [1–2]Supply the verb phrase **ōrō vōs faciātis**. [3]**ego**: a new sentence begins here. [4]**Astylus**: the name of the sign painter.

16. 425; IX, ?, ?; Via di Nola.

Claudium
IIvir · animula · facit

The date of candidacy is unknown. [2]**animula**: note the diminutive formation as a term of endearment.

17. 429; IX, ?, ?; Via di Nola.

C · Iulium · Polybium
aed · ovf · panem · bonum · fert

Polybius was a candidate for the office of aedile in the last ten years of the city. [2]**panem**: starts a new sentence.

18. 456; V, ?, ?; Via di Nola.

A · Vettium
Firmum · verecundissimum
iuvenem · d · v · a · s · p · p · o · v · faciatis

For the date of the candidacy, see I, 1, 6. [3]**d · v · a · s · p · p**: abbrev. for **duumvirum viīs aedīlibus sacrīs pūblicīsque prōcūrandīs**, which is another way of referring to the office of aedile. [3]**iuvenem**: this noun refers to men up to the age of 45.

19. 485; V, ?, ?; Via di Nola.

Marcel[l]um · aed · lignari
plostrari · rog · Lassi
cum · [F]abio · et · Crimio · et ·
C · Nisio I[n]fantione
ubiq ·

If **Mārcellum** refers to **Cn. Casellius Marcellus**, see I, 1, 9. [1-2]**lignārī, plōstrārī**: §2.2 2nd Declension Nominative/Vocative Plural. **lignārī (et) plōstrārī** are subjects of **rogant**. [2]**plōstrārī**: note the spelling with **ō**, cf. **plaustrārī** and §2.1 Monophthongization. [2]**Lassī**: gentilicium, nom. pl. masc. of Lassius. The plural refers to members of the family. Supply the verb **rogant**. [5]**ubiq**: abbrev. for **ubique**.

20. 499; VII, iv, 15; Via del Foro.

[Cn · Alle]ium · Maium · d · v · i · d
Aurelius · civem · bonum · fac

The date of Maius' candidacy is unknown. [1]**[Cn]**: abbrev. for **Gnaeum**. [2]**cīvem · bonum**: in apposition to **[Cn · Allē]ium · Māium**. [2]**fac**: abbrev. for **facit**.

21. 575; VII, ii, 41–42; Via degli Augustali.

Vatiam · aed · rogant
Macerio · dormientes
universi · cum
[– – –]

For the date of the candidacy, see I, 1, 3. This electoral announcement makes light of the candidacy of **Vatia**. [1]**rogant**: the subject is **Macerīō (et) dormientēs ūniversī cum . . .** [2]**dormientēs**: '(those) behaving as if asleep; idle.' [4]The final portion of the inscription is not legible.

22. 581; VII, ii, 43–44; Via degli Augustali.

M · Cerrinium
Vatiam · aed · ovf · seri · bibi
universi · rogant
scr · Florus · cum · Fructo · [– – –]

For the date of the candidacy, see I, 1, 3. This inscription also makes light of the candidacy of **Marcus Cerrinius Vatia**. His supporters are those who carouse late into the night. [2]**seri · bibī**: even though **seri** and **bibī** are separated by a word punct, they belong together as members of a compound word **seribibī**, 'late night drinkers.' [4]**Flōrus**: name of the sign painter. [4]**Fructō**: probably the name of the **dealbātor**, 'whitewasher.'

23. 597; VII, ii, 51–52; Via degli Augustali.

Suettios · Certum · IIvir · i · d ·
Verum · aed · Celsum · collegam · rog ·

quorum · innocentiam
probastis
Elainus · dissign · rog

The candidates are generally placed in the second half of the 70s AD. [1]**Suettiōs**: accusative plural of the family name **Suettius**; **Certum** (line 1) and **Verum** (line 2) are cognomina. The inscription refers, then, to two members of the **Suettius** family, *viz.*, **Suettium Certum** and **Suettium Verum**, who were standing for the duumvirate. Their colleague, **Celsus**, was standing for the office of the aedile. [2]**rog**: abbrev. for **rogāmus**. [3]**innocentiam**: 'integrity.' [4]**probāstis**: 2nd pl. perf. This is a so-called syncopated perfect form. The full form is **probāvistis**. For discussion see §2.3 Perfect Tense. [5]**dissign**: abbrev. for **dissignātor**, a word which refers to an official who assigned seats at theatrical shows or who presided over funerary ceremonies.

24. 635; VII, xii, 14; Via degli Augustali.

Sabinum · aed
Procule · fac · et · ille
te · faciet

[1]**Sabīnum**: probably **Marcus Epidius Sabinus**, whose candidacy may be placed in the first half of the 70s AD. [2]**Procule**: it is possible that **Proculus** is the candidate mentioned in I, 1, 28.

25. 698; VIII, i, 2; Basilica; Via Marina.

Sabinum · et · Rufum ·
aed · d · r · p · Valentinus · cum
discentes · suos · rog

For the full name of **Sabinus** and the date of his candidacy, see note on I, 1, 24. Note that this announcement is for a pair of candidates. [1]**Rufum**: his full name is **Quintus Marius Rufus**. [2]**aed · d · r · p**: abbrev. for **aedīlēs dignōs reī pūblicae**. [2–3]**cum discentēs suōs**: §2.4 Prepositions. For the meaning of **discentēs**, see I, 1, 12.

26. 768; VIII, i, 11–12; Via dell'Abbondanza.

M · Epidium · Sabinum · d · i · dic ·

2 **ovf**
3 **dig · est**
4 **defensorem · coloniae · ex · sententia · Suedi · Clementis · sancti · iudicis**
5 **consensu · ordinis · obmerita · eius · et · probitatem · dignum · rei publicae · faciat**
6 **Sabinus · dissignator · cum · plausu · facit**

If **Sabinus** stood for the office of aedile in the first half of the 70s AD, then this inscription, in which he stands for the duumvirate, belongs to the final years of the city, since there must have been a period of time between candidacies. The syntax of this inscription is difficult. Lines 2–3 of this text were painted in smaller letters to the right of line 1. They should be taken as independent sentences. [1]**d · i · dīc**: abbrev. for **duumvirum iūrē dīcendō**. [4]**dēfēnsōrem · colōniae**: in apposition to **M · Epidium · Sabīnum** (line 1), which is itself the direct object of the verb **faciāt** (= **faciātis)** in line 5. [3]**dig**: abbrev. for **dignus**. [4]**colōniae**: This word refers to the city of Pompeii, which was settled by veterans of the army of Sulla in 80 BC. **Suedī**: gen. sg. of the gentilicium, **Suedius**. Suedius Clemens was sent to Pompeii by the emperor Nero after the earthquake of A.D. 62 in order to settle disputes involving the illegal appropriation and use of public lands. [4]**sānctī**: probably in the sense 'scrupulous, upright,' but 'sacrosanct (by virtue of appointment)' is also possible. [4]**iūdicis**: here perhaps 'arbiter.' [5]**ōrdinis**: This refers to the Pompeiian town council, which consisted of approximately 100 prominent citizens and which was responsible for overseeing much of the town's business. [5]**obmerita**: the prepositional phrase **ob merita** was written as a single word because the preposition **ob** was proclitic to the noun (**merita**) that it governed. [5]**faciat**: abbrev. for **faciātis**. Supply **ōrō vōs**. [6]**plausū**: 'with the approval (of the town council and **Suedius Clemens**).'

27. 787; VIII, iv, 32–33; Via del Tempio di Iside.

1 **Cn · Helvium**
2 **Sabinum · aed · Isiaci**
3 **universi · rog**

For the date of the candidacy see I, 1, 14. [2]**Īsiācī**: 'worshipers in the cult of Isis.' The temple of Isis, of which there are significant remains standing today, is located at VIII, vii, 28.

28. 1048; I, iv, 19–20; Via dell'Abbondanza.

Q · P · P · iuvenem
aed · ovf · d · r · p
Sabinus · rog · copo

[1]**Q · P · P**: abbrev. for **Quīntum Postumium Proculum**. His candidacy belongs to the final 10 years of the city. [1]**iuvenem**: technically, this noun refers to an adult male up to the age of 45. [2]**d · r · p**: abbrev. for **dignum reī pūblicae**. **dignum** modifies **Proculum**. [3]**Sabīnus**: begins a news sentence. [3]**rog**: the direct object is **Proculum**. [3]**cōpō**: §2.1 Monophthongization, cf. **caupō**. **cōpō** is in apposition to the name **Sabīnus**.

29. 1059; IX, i, 20; Via dell'Abbondanza.

M · Epidium
Sabinum
II vir · iur · dic · o · v · f · dignum · iuvenem
Suedius · Clemens · sanctissimus
iudex · facit · vicinis · rogantibus

For the date of the candidacy, see I, 1, 26. [3]**iūr · dīc**: abbrev. for **iūrē dīcendō**. [3]**dignum · iuvenem**: in apposition to **Sabīnum**. [4]**Suedius Clemēns**: begins a new sentence. For **Suedius** see I, 1, 26. [5]**facit**: the direct object is **Sabīnum**. [5]**vīcīnīs rogantibus**: abl. of accompaniment.

30. 1147; II, iv, 5–7; Via dell'Abbondanza.

A · Vettium · Firmum
aed · o · v · f · d · r · p · o · v · f · pilicrepi · facite

For the date of the candidacy, see I, 1, 6. [2]**pilicrepī**: voc. pl. masc. The meaning of this compound (**pili-** + **-crepus**) is uncertain. 'Ballplayer' or 'scorer' are possibilities.

31. 2887; VII, iv, 44;; Vicolo Storto.

Quintio · si qui · recusat
assidat ad asinum

[– – –]fa[– – –]

[1]**Quīntio**: probably stands for **Quīnctio**, acc. sg. masc. The spelling of the accusative with **o** instead of **u** is not unusual at Pompeii. **Quīnctio** is direct object of **recūsat**. §2.1 Word-final Consonants: **m**. [1]**quī**: note the form of the interrogative-indefinite pronoun. Interrogative-indefinite **quī** arose from **quis** by sound change before words beginning with voiced sounds, e.g., **quis vocat** > **quī vocat**. Compare the form of the prefix **dis-** in **dīvellō**, which comes from **disvellō*. This change is the source of the confusion with the relative pronoun, **quī**. Interrogative-indefinite **quī** is well attested in Old Latin authors, e.g., Plautus, Cato, and is found also in late Republican/early imperial period writers such as Cicero, Vergil, Horace, and Ovid. [2]**assīdat**: subjunctive of **assīdō, -ere** 'to sit down, take a seat.' [2]**asinum**: the idea seems to be that the voter should sit next to the ass in order to be whipped for his stubbornness as is an ass. [3]The letters painted in this line have all but vanished.

32. 3409; V, i, 18;; Via del Vesuvio.

Popidium · Secundum
aed · d · r · p · probissimum · iuvenem · ovf
Rufine · fave · et · ille · te faciet

This candidacy is dated to AD 79. [2]**d · r · p · probissimum · iuvenem**: these phrases go with **Secundum**.

33. 3433; V, i, 27; Via del Vesuvio.

Ceium · Secundum
II vir · Q · S · Caecili · Iucundi rogam

The candidacy of **Lūcius Ceius Secundus** is generally assigned to the second half of the 70s AD. [2]**Caecilī · Iūcundī**: nom. pl. masc. The two praenomina, **Quīntus** and **Sextus**, refer to brothers from the family of **Caecilius Iūcundus**. **rogām**: abbrev. for **rogāmus**.

34. 3502; VI, xiv, 39; Vicolo dei Vetti.

[Holc]onium · Priscum aed · Clodi · fac ·
Sei · copo · probe · fecisti

quod · sella · commodasti

For the candidate, see inscription I, 1, 2. The date at which he stood for the office of aedile may be assigned to the early 70s AD. Lines 2 and 3 are written in smaller letters to the right of line 1. [1]**Clōdī**: voc. sg. masc. [2]**Sēī**: voc. sg. masc. of the name **Sēius**. [2]**cōpō**: voc. sg. masc. §2.1 Monophthongization. [3]**sella**: acc. sg. fem. §2.1 Word-final Consonants: **m**. [3]**commodāstī**: 2nd sg. perf. §2.3 Perfect Tense. The inscription is divided into two syntactic units. The first sentence is line 1. Lines 2 and 3 form the second sentence. The meaning of the **quod**-clause is not entirely clear. Some scholars think that **Sēius**, the innkeeper, provided the sign painter with a chair or stool so that he could rest after painting (the announcement is located too high on the wall for the **scrīptor** to have painted while he was seated).

35. 3527; VI, xv, 3; Vicolo dei Vettii.

Pupium ·
IIvir · i d ovf · Appuleia
cum · Mustio · vicino · f
et · Narcissus · vos · roga[nt]

[1]**Pupium**: for the candidate, see I, 1, 36. The date of this candidacy is unknown. [2]**Appulēia**: starts a new sentence. [3]**f**: abbrev. for **fullōne**. For the occupation of **Mustius**, see the following inscription. Both **vīcīnō** and **fullōne** are in apposition to **Mustiō**.

36. 3529; VI, xv, 3; Vicolo dei Vettii.

M · Pupium · Rufum ·
II · vir · i · d · dignum · r · [p] ovf
Mustius · fullo · facit
et · dealbat · scr · unicus
s[in]e · reliq · sodalib · non[– – –]

Compare I, 1, 35. [4]**dēalbat · scr**: asyndeton. [5]**reliq · sodalib**: abbrev. for **reliquīs sodālibus**. [5]**non[– – –]**: the remainder of the inscription is illegible. Most commentators think that **non[** is to be restored as **Nōn[īs]** and that this portion of the text indicates the date on which the announcement was painted. This seems unlikely since there are no other electoral announcements in which the date of the painting is specified.

37. 3702; IX, vi, 8; Vicolo del Centenario.

1 **Bruttium · Balbum**
2 **· II · vir**
3 **· Gen[ialis]**
4 **r**
5 **hic · aerarium · conservabit**

The date of this candidacy is uncertain. Lines 2 and 3 and 4 are painted in smaller letters to the right of lines 1 and 5. ^{4}**r**: abbrev. for **rogat**. The subject is **Gen[iālis]**. ^{5}**hic**: nom. sg. masc. The pronoun refers to **Bruttius Balbus**. ^{5}**aerārium**: the public treasury at Pompeii.

38. 3738; IX, vii, 2–3; Via dell'Abbondanza.

1 **L Popidium Secundum**
2 **aed · o v f · Rustius face scrib[– – –]**

For this candidate, see I, 1, 32. ^{2}**face**: 3rd sg. pres. act. Some speakers at Pompeii did not pronounce word-final **t**. The change of **i** to **e** in final syllables is common in graffiti. Compare **facit** and see §2.1 Short **i** and §2.1 Word-final Consonants: **t**. ^{2}**scrīb[– – –]**: the rest of the inscription is illegible and so the subject of **scrīb[it]** can not be determined.

39. 3741. X, vii, 2–3; Via dell' Abbondanza.

1 **Claudium Verum**
2 **II · v · i · d · o · v · f · iuvenem integr**

The date of the candidacy cannot be determined. ^{2}**integr**: abbrev. for **integrum**.

40. 3771; IX, viii, 6; Via di Nola.

1 **N · Herennium · Celsum**
2 **d · v · v · a · s · p · p · d · r · p · o · v · f · [d] · est**

The date of this candidacy is probably to be assigned to the final years of the city. [2]**d · v · v · a · s · p · p**: abbrev. for **duumvirum viīs aedibus sacrīs pūblicīs prōcūrandīs**. [2]**[d]**: abbrev. for **dignus**.

41. 3775; IX, vii, 8; Via dell'Abbondanza.

L Statium · Receptum
II · vir · i · d · o · v · f · vicini · dig ·
scr · Aemilius · Celer · vic ·
invidiose
qui · deles
ae[g]rotes

The date of the candidacy is unknown. This dipinto has 3 parts: (1) Lines 1 and 2 form the electoral announcement. (2) Line 3 refers to the sign painter. (3) Lines 4–6 form a warning to those who deface announcements. [2]**vīcīnī**: voc. pl. masc. [2]**dig**: abbrev. for **dignus**. Supply the verb **est**. The subject is **Lūcius Statius Receptus**. [3]**scr**: abbrev. for **scrībit**. [3]**vīc**: abbreviation for **vīcīnus**. This noun stands in apposition to **Aemilius Celer**. [4]**invidiōse**: voc. sg. masc. It's also possible to take this word as the adverb **invidiōsē**. [6]**ae[g]rōtēs**: subjunctive.

42. 6626; V, iv, a; Vicolo di M. Lucretius Fronto.

si · pudor · in vita quicquam · prodesse · putatur
Lucretius · hic · Fronto · dignus · honore · bono · est

The electoral announcement is composed in the form of an elegiac couplet but there are some metrical improprieties. In line 2 **Lucrētius** does not scan as a dactyl. The break separating the two halves of the pentameter falls after the name **Frontō**. Note also aphaeresis of **e** in the verb **est** (line 2). Scan as an iamb **bonō (e)st**. [1]**quicquam**: internal accusative with **prōdesse**. Translate as 'to be of any use.' [2]**hic**: nom. masc. sg. in apposition to **Lucrētius Frontō**. [2]**dignus**: governs the ablative case.

43. 7197; I, vii, 1; Via dell'Abbondanza.

P · Paquium · Proculum
[du]umvirum · i · d · vicini · cupidi · faciunt

For the date of the candidacy see I, 1, 11.

44. 7201; I, vii, 1; Via dell'Abbondanza.

C · Cuspium · aed
si · qua · verecunde · viventi · gloria · danda · est
huic · iuveni · debet · gloria · dari

[1]**C · Cuspium**: **Gāius Cuspius Pānsa**. His candidacy is dated to the final year of the city. [1]**aed**: supply the verb phrase **ōrō vōs faciātis**. [2]**qua**: indefinite pronominal adjective, nom. sg. fem., modifying **glōria**. Line 2 scans as a dactylic hexameter. There is aphaeresis of **e** in the verb **est**. The words at the beginning of line 3, **huic iuvenī dēbet**, scan as the first two and a half feet of a pentameter.

45. 7203; I, vii, 1; Via dell'Abbondanza.

M · Epidium
Sabinum d i d ovf
sanctus · ordo · facit
Suedio · Clementi · sancto · iudici
feliciter

For the candidate, see I, 1, 26 and I, 1, 29. [3]**sānctus**: starts a new sentence. [4]**Suediō · Clementī · sānctō · iūdicī**: the datives depend on **fēlīciter** in line 5. For **Suedius** see I, 1, 26 and I, 1, 29. [5]**fēlīciter**: adverb used elliptically with the meaning 'good luck.'

46. 7221; I, vii, 3; Via dell'Abbondanza.

L Popidium · aed · Ismurna · rog

L Popidium: either **Lūcius Popidius Secundus** or **Lūcius Popidius Ampliātus**. For **Popidius Secundus** see I, 1, 32 and I, 1, 38; for **Popidius Ampliātus** see I, 1, 52 and I, 1, 53. **Ismurna**: cognomen of Greek origin, cf. **Smyrna**. This is the only example at Pompeii of the insertion (so-called prothesis) of a vowel before word-initial clusters of **s** plus consonant. This feature is well attested in other areas of the Roman empire, cf. **istatuam**, acc. sg. fem., 'statue', *CIL* XI 5996.

47. 7242; I, vii, 7; Via dell' Abbondanza.

1 **C · Gavium · Rufum · M · Holconium · Priscum**
2 **IIvir · i · d · ovf**
3 **Cuspium · Pansam · Popidium · Secundum · aediles · d · r · p · o · v · f**

These men stood for office in AD 79. See I, 1, 2 for **Holcōnius Priscus** and **Gāvius Rufus**; I, 1, 12 and I, 1, 44 for **Cuspius Pānsa**. See I, 1, 34 for **Holcōnius Priscus'** candidacy for the office of aedile.

48. 7273; I, viii, 7; Via dell' Abbondanza.

1 **Cn · Helvium · Sabinum · aed**
2 **pistores · rog · et cupiunt · cum · vicinis**

For the candidate, see I, 1, 27.

49. 7605; III, i, 6; Via dell'Abbondanza.

1 **Epidium · Sabinum**
2 **II vir · iur · dic · o · v · f · Trebius · cliens · facit**
3 **consentiente · sanctissimo**
4 **ordine**

For the candidate see I, 1, 26; I, 1, 29; and I, 1, 43. [3–4]**cōnsentiente · sānctissimō ōrdine**: ablative absolute.

50. 7619; III, ii, 1; Via dell'Abbondanza.

1 **Trebi · surge · fac**
2 **aed · Lollium · Fuscum**
3 **adulescentem · probum**

The candidacy of **C. Lollius Fuscus** belongs to the last ten years of the city. [1]**Trebī**: voc. sg. masc. of **Trebius**. **Aulus Trebius Valens** stood as a candidate for the office of aedile in the first half of the 70s AD. [1]**surge · fac**: asyndeton. [3]**adulescentem**: compare the use of **iuvenis** to describe younger candidates.

51. 7621; III, ii, 1; Via dell'Abbondanza.

C · Iulium Polybium
aed v a s p p
lanternari · tene
scalam

For the date of Polybius' candidacy, see I, 1, 17. [3]**lanternārī**: voc. sg. masc. [4]**scālam**: this word is rarely found in the singular.

52. 7650; III, iii, 2; Via dell'Abbondanza.

Ampliatum · aed · dignus
est · Graphicae · dormis
et · cupis

[1]**Ampliātum**: refers to **Lūcius Popidius Ampliātus** (see I, 1, 52 and I, 1, 55). **Popidius Ampliātus** may also be mentioned in I, 1, 46. His candidacy probably belongs to the last ten years of the city. [1]**aed**: supply the verb phrase **ōrō vōs faciātis**. [2]**Graphicae**: voc. sg. masc. of **Graphicus**, a cognomen of Greek origin. For the spelling of short **e** by means of **ae**, see §2.1 Monophthongization.

53. 7665; III, iii, 6; Via dell' Abbondanza.

L · Popidium · L · f · Ampliatum
aed · d · r · p · et · coloniae · Pompeianae · o · v · f
Infanticulus cum sodalibus · rog

For the candidate, see I, 1, 52 and I, 1, 55. [1]**L**: abbrev. of **Lūcī**, gen. sg. masc. [1]**f**: abbrev. for **fīlium**, acc. sg. masc. Mention of filiation is rare in electoral announcements. [2]**d**: abbrev. for **dignum**. The adjective governs **r(eī) p(ūblicae)** and **colōniae Pompeiānae**.

54. 7676; III, iv, 1; Via dell' Abbondanza.

L · Ceium · Secundum · IIvir
o · v · f · d · r · p · Urblanenses · rog

[Facsimile 11] For the candidacy of **Secundus**, see I, 1, 33. [2]**Urblānēnsēs**: syncope of medial **u**. §2.1 Syncope. This word refers to inhabitants of the neighborhood **Urbulānum**, which was probably located in the area near the Porta di Nola.

55. 7851; IX, vii, 9; Via dell'Abbondanza.

1 **L · Popidium · L · f · Ampliatum**
2 **aed · Montanus cliens**
3 **rogat · cum · latruncularis**

For the candidate, see I, 1, 52 and I, 1, 53. [1]**L · f**: see I, 1, 53. [3]**latrunculārīs**: §2.3 Dative/Ablative Plural.

56. 7863; IX, xi, 2; Via dell'Abbondanza.

1 **C · Lollium**
2 **Fuscum II · vir · v · a · s · p · p**
3 **Asellinas rogant**
4 **nec · sine · Zmyrina**

For the candidacy, see I, 1, 50. [3]**Asellinas**: nom. pl. fem. The source of this unusual ending is best explained as showing the use of accusative for nominative, a feature which is attested sporadically in Latin from the first century AD, e.g., **linguas**, nom. pl. fem., on a curse tablet from Africa. [4]**nec**: here with the function of the negator **nōn**. [4]**Zmyrinā**: cognomen of Greek origin, cf. **Smyrna**, and note the spelling **Ismurna** in I, 1, 46. The **i** here is an epenthetic vowel. For epenthetic vowels in other Greek loanwords see II, 9, 207.

57. Giordano & Casale 14; I, xvi, 5; ?.

1 **L · C · Secundum**
2 **II · vir · i · d · o · v · f · Petronia · cupide · rogat**

For the candidacy of **Secundus**, see I, 1, 33. [1]**C**: note the abbreviation of the nomen and compare with I, 1, 28 where all names were abbreviated.

2. Gladiatorial Announcements

58. 1180; VIII, vii, 20; Teatro grande.

1 **pro salute**
2 **[imp · Vespasiani ·] Caesaris · Augu[sti] li[b]e[ro]rumqu[e]**
3 **[eius · et · ob ·] dedicationem · ara<e> · [fam · gladiat ·] Cn · [All]ei · Nigidi · Mai**
4 **flami[nis ·] Caesaris · Augusti · pugn · Pompeis · sine · ulla · dilatione**
5 **III · Non · Iul · venatio vela erunt**

Gladiatorial contests offered to commemorate the dedication of an altar in front of the temple of Vespasian. [2]**[imp · Vespasiānī ·] Caesaris · Augu[sti]**: Vespasian was emperor from AD 69–79, so that provides a chronological frame for the date of the inscription. [2]**imp**: abbrev. for **imperātōris.** [2]**li[b]e[ro]rumqu[e]**: Vespasian had three children. Titus, who was the elder son, Domitian and a daughter named Flavia Domitilla. [3]**ara<e>**: the inscription reads **aram.** [3]**[fam · gladiat ·]**: abbrev. for **familia gladiātōria.** [3]**Cn · [All]eī Nigidī Māī:** see I, 1, 20 for **Maius**' political candidacy. [4]**pugn**: abbrev. for **pugnābit.** [5]**III · Nōn · Iūl**: = **tertiō diē Nōnās Iūliās.** [5]**vēnātiō vēla**: asyndeton. These words begin a new sentence.

59. 1186; VIII, vii; 20; large theater.

1 **N · Popidi**
2 **Rufi · fam · glad · [p]u[g]n · Pompeis · venati[o]**
3 **ex · XII · K · Mai · mala · <e>t · vela · erunt**
4 **o · procurator**
5 **felicitas**

[1]**N**: abbrev. for **Numerī**, gen. sg. masc. of praenomen **Numerius. Numerius Popidius Rufus** was a candidate for the duumvirate in the last ten years of the city. This **ēdictum** then belongs to the last decade of the life of the city. [3]**ex · XII · K · Mai**: = **ex diē duodecimō ante Kalendās Māiās.** [3]**mala**: it is not clear what this word refers to, if indeed this is the correct reading. The idea that it means 'apples' and that these were distributed as a donative at the games does not have much to recommend it. [3]**<e>t**: only **t** is written. The syntax of the first three lines is difficult. However, since **vēnātiō et vēla**

erunt is a common concluding sentence in gladiatorial announcements, it seems best to take **vēnāti[ō]** at the end of line 2 with **mala <e>t · vēla · erunt** in line 3. [4–5]These lines are not part of the gladiatorial announcement. [4]**prōcūrātor**: refers to an official who managed one of the **lūdī** or gladiatorial schools. [5]**fēlīcitās**: supply dative pronoun **tibi**.

60. 1189; VIII, iii, 1; Via dell' Abbondanza.

A · Suetti · Cer[t]i
aedilis · familia · gladiatoria · pugnab · Pompeis
pr · K · Iunias · venatio · et · vela · erunt

Aulus Suettius Certus was a candidate for the duumvirate in the final years of the city. We do not know when he served as aedile. [1]**A**: abbrev. for **Aulī**, gen. sg. masc. of the praenomen **Aulus**. [2]**pugnāb**: abbrev. for **pugnābit**. [3]**pr · K · Iūniās**: abbrev. for **prīdiē Kalendās Iūniās**. [3]**vēnātiō**: begin a new sentence here.

61. 1190; VII, i, 42–43 or VII, xii, 15; Vico del Lupanare.

A · Suetti · Cer[t]i
aedilis · familia · gladiatoria · pugnabit · Pompeis
pr · K · Iunias · venatio · et · vela · erunt
omnibus · Nero[n · mun]eribus · feliciter
lanifricari
dormis
scr
Secundus
de · albante · Vic[tor]e
adstante
Vesbino
· em[. . .]tore
[. . .]ri[. . .]o

The contest referred to in this dipinto is the same as that announced in I, 2, 60. This text has four parts: (1) lines 1–3 form the gladiatorial announcement; (2) line 4 is a salute to the shows put on by members of a gladiatorial school known as **Nerōniānī**; (3) lines 5–6 seems to be an aside addressed to an acquaintance of the sign-painter; (4) lines 7–11 refer to the painter and his assistants. Lines 12 and 13 are too illegible to permit interpretation. [3]**pr · K ·**

Iūniās: = **prīdiē Kalendās Iūniās**. [4]**Nerō[n]**: abbrev. for **Nerōniānōrum**. [5]**lānifricārī**: voc. sg. masc. [9]**dē · albante**: abl. sg. masc. Despite the word punct, these two forms are constitutents of a compound **dēalbante**; cf. I, 1, 11. [10]**adstante**: abl. sg. masc., 'assistant.'

62. 3881; necropolis, Porta di Nocera; Via di Nocera.

glad · par · XX Q · Monni
Rufi · pug · No<l>a · K · Mais · VI ·
V · Nonas · Maias · et
venatio · erit

Notice for gladiatorial contests to take place at Nola, a Campanian town north of Pompeii. The dipinto cannot be dated but it is attributed by some to the first quarter of the imperial period. [1]**glad · par**: abbrev. for **gladiātōrum paria**. [2]**pug**: abbrev. for **pugnābunt**. [2]**No<l>ā**: the inscription has **Noiā**. Abl. sg. fem. with locative function. See §2.4 Ablative for Locative. [2]**K**: abbrev. for **Kalendīs**. [2]**Māīs**: abl. pl. fem. [2–3]**VI · V · Nōnās · Māiās**: = **diē sextō, diē quīntō ante Nōnās Māiās**.

63. 3882; necropolis, Porta di Nocera; Via di Nocera.

numini
Augustali
glad · par · XX · et · venatio · <St>a Pompei · flaminis
Augustalis
pugnab · Constant · Nucer · III · pr · Non
Non · VIII · Eidus · Maias
Nucerini · officia · mea · certo · index

Notice for gladiatorial contests to take place at Nuceria, a Campanian town located east of Pompeii. The dipinto can not be dated accurately, but is probably to be placed in the period before the earthquake of AD 62, since this gate seems not to have been in use after the earthquake. [1–2]**nūminī Augustālī**: dat. sg. masc.; translate 'for the divine nature of the emperor.' [3]**vēnātiō**: seems to refer here to a 'company of animal fighters,' rather than the spectacle itself. [3]**<St>a**: *CIL* IV prints **da** here, but one expects the praenomen of **Pompēius**. Still, **<St>a** is not the usual abbreviation for **Statius**. [3]**Pompeī**: this is the family name of the **flāmen Augustālis**. **Pompēius** is the sponsor of the games. [5]**Cōnstant · Nūcer**: abbrev. for **Cōnstantiae Nūceriae**, loc. sg. fem., the town of Nuceria. [5-6]**III · pr · Nōn**

Nōn VIII Eidūs Māiās: abbrev. for **diē tertiō ante Nōnās Māiās, prīdiē Nōnās Māiās, Nōnīs Māīs, diē octāvō ante Eidūs Māiās.** [6]**Eidūs**: the letters **Ei** spell long **ī**. See §2.1 Long Vowels. [7]**Nūcerīnī:** voc. pl. masc., 'inhabitants of Nuceria.' [7]**certo · index**: the meaning of these words and thus the meaning of line 7 are unclear.

64. 3884; IX, viii, 4; Via di Nola.

1 **D · Lucreti ·**
2 **Satri · Valentis · flaminis · Neronis · Caesaris · Aug fili**
3 **perpetui · gladiatorum · paria · XX · et · D · Lucreti{ō} · Valentis fili**
4 **glad · paria · X · pug · Pompeis · VI · V · IV · III · pr · Idus Apr · venatio · legitima ·**
5 **et · vela · erunt**
6 **scr**
7 **Aemilius**
8 **Celer sing**
9 **ad luna**
10 **scr**
11 **Celer**

Decimus Lucrētius Satrius Valēns was a candidate for the office of aedile in A.D. 69 so this dipinto can be dated to the last decade of the city. This inscription has two parts: (1) the gladiatorial announcement, lines 1–5; (2) the 'signature' of the painter, lines 6-11. Lines 10–11, which are painted inside of the **c** of **Lucrētī** in line 1, repeat the name of the painter, given in 6–9. [1]**D**: abbrev. for **Decimī**, praenomen, gen. sg. masc. [2]**flāminis**: in apposition to **D · Lucrētī Satrī · Valentis.** [2]**Aug**: abbrev. for **Augustī**. [2]**fīlī**: in apposition to **Nerōnis · Caesaris.** [3]**perpetuī**: the adjective modifies **flāminis**. [3]**Lucrētī{ō}**: misspelling for **Lucrētī**, gen. sg. masc. [4]**glad**: abbrev. for **gladiātōrum**. [4]**VI · V · IV · III · pr · Īdūs Apr**: abbrev. for **diē sextō ante Īdūs Aprīlēs, diē quīntō ante Īdūs Aprīlēs, diē quārtō ante Īdūs Aprīlēs, diē tertiō Īdūs Aprīlēs, prīdiē Īdūs Aprīlēs.** [4]**lēgitima**: 'prescribed by custom.' The idea seems to be that a **vēnātiō** is the customary way to end the games. [8]**sing**: abbrev. for **singulus**, 'alone.' [9]**ad lūna**: acc. sg. fem., 'by moonlight.'

65. 7989; II, vii; Palestra grande.

1 **pro · salute**
2 **Neronis · Claudi · Caesaris · Aug · Germanici · Pompeis · Ti · Claudi · Veri · venatio**
3 **athletae · et · sparsiones · er<u>nt · V · IIII · <K> · Mart C · CCLXXIII**
4 **Celer · lorarius · Maio · delibat**
5 **Maio · principi · coloniae · felic**
6 **Claudio Vero · felic**

Tiberius Claudius Verus was duumvir in AD 61, which could then be the date for this dipinto. This fits in well with the fact that no gladiatorial combats are advertised. Gladiatorial combats were not permitted at Pompeii for several years after the riot in AD 59. This inscription has 4 syntactic units: (1) lines 1-3; (2) line 4; (3) line 5; (4) line 6. [2]The emperor's name is **Nerō Claudius Caesar Augustus Germānicus**. [3]**er<u>nt**: corrected from **erint**, although the possibility of an analogical formation based on the future stem **eri-** is a slim possibility. [3]**V · IIII · <K> · Mārt**: abbrev. for **diē quīntō ante Kalendās Mārtiās, diē quārtō ante Kalendās Mārtiās**. [3]**<K>**: the inscription reads **F**, which must be an error. [3]**C · CCLXXIII**: probably refers to the amount of money to be distributed as **sparsiōnēs** at the gladiatorial contests. Translate as a separate sentence: '373 (sesterces will be distributed).' [4]**lōrārius**: 'a harness-maker,' but here perhaps a type of gladiator who fights with leather tongs. [4]**dēlībat**: 'pour a libation to' + dat. [5]**Māiō**: dat. sg. masc. referring to **Gnaeus Allēius Nigidius Māius**, a sponsor of gladiatorial shows (see I, 2, 58). [6]**fēlīc**: abbrev. for **fēlīciter**, 'good luck.'

66. 7991; III, ii, 1; Via dell'Abbondanza.

1 **Cn · Allei · Nigidi**
2 **Mai quinq · sine · impensa · publica · glad · par · XX · et · eorum · supp · pugn · Pompeis**
3 **Gavillius Tigillo**
4 **et · Clodio · sal**
5 **Telephe · summa · rudis**
6 **instrumentum · muneris**
7 **u · va**
8 **Diadumeno · et · Pyladioni fel**

[Facsimile 12] For the candidacy of **Gnaeus Allēius Nigidius Māius**, see I, 1, 20. See also I, 2, 58. The date of this inscription is uncertain. **Māius** was quinquennial duumvir in AD 55, but this inscription is not likely to be that old. Lines 3–8 are painted to the right of lines 1–2 and do not form part of the gladiatorial announcement. This dipinto has four constituents: The gladiatorial announcement is lines 1–2. Lines 3–4 are a salute to **Tigillus** and **Clōdius**. Lines 5–7 form a salute to Telephus, a gladiatorial instructor or referee. Line 8 is an expression of good luck, perhaps for two gladiators, **Diadumenus** and **Pyladiō**. [2]**quīnq**: abbrev. for **quīnquennālis**, 'quinquennial duumvir,' gen. sg. masc. [2]**supp**: abbrev. for **suppositīcī**. [4]**sal**: abbrev. for **salūtem**. Supply the verb **dīcit**. [5]**summa rudis**: title given to head instructor of a gladiatorial school. This term is also used for the referee of a gladiatorial contest. [6]**īnstrumentum mūneris**: in apposition to **summa rudis**. [7]**u**: abbrev. for **ubīque**. [7]**va**: abbrev. for **valē**.

67. 7992; III, ii, 1; Via dell'Abbondanza.

1 **D · Lucreti · Satri**
2 **Valentis · flaminis · [[Neronis]] · Caesaris · Aug · f · perpetui · glad · par · XX · et · D · Lucreti · Valentis · fili**
3 **glad · par · X · pugn · Pompeis · ex · a · d · Nonis · Apr · venatio · et · vela · erunt**
4 **Poly**

For the sponsor, see I, 2, 64. [2]**[[Nerōnis]]**: the name was covered with limestone, which is an indication that it was intentionally erased, a case of *damnatio memoriae*. [2]**f**: abbrev. for **fīlī**, gen. sg. masc. [4]**ex · a · d · Nonis · Apr**: abbrev. for **ex ante diem Nōnīs Aprilibus**, which stands for **ex ante diem Nōnās Aprīlēs**. Note that the prepositional phrase **ante diem Nōnās Aprīlēs** is the object of **ex**. **Poly**: abbrev. for **Polybius**, name of the sign painter.

68. 7993; III, ii, 1; Via dell'Abbondanza.

1 **dedicatione**
2 **operis · tabularum · Cn · Allei · Nigidi · Mai · Pompeis · Idibus · Iunis**
3 **pompa · venatio · athletae vela · erunt**
4 **Nigra · va**

5 **Ocella**

See I, 2, 58 and I, 2, 66. [2]**operis · tabulārum**: this phrase refers to painted tablets, perhaps commemorating the gladiatorial contests sponsored by **Māius**. [3]**pompa**: gladiatorial contests began with a festive procession that included the sponsor (**ēditor**) of the contests, his assistants, the gladiatorial contestants, lictors, trumpeters (**tubicenēs**), and so forth. [4]**Nigra**: voc. sg. [5]**Ocella**: this name is painted inside the **o** of **dedicātiōne**, line 1, and refers to the painter.

69. 7994; III, iv, 1–2; Via dell'Abbondanza.

1 **par · XLIX**
2 **familia · Capiniana · muneri[bus]**
3 **Augustor<u>m · pug · Puteol · a · d · IV · Idus M[aias]**
4 **pr · Id · Mai · et · XVII · XV · K · Iu[nias]**
5 **vela · erit Magus**

Notice for gladiatorial contests at Puteoli. The dipinto cannot be dated. [1]**par**: abbrev. for **paria**. Supply **gladiātōrum**. [2]**familiā Capiniānā**: abl. sg. fem. **Capiniānā** refers to the entrepreneur (**lanista**), Capinius, who supplied the contestants and animals for the games. [3]**Augustōr<u>m**: the inscription has **Augustōrm**. If this dipinto belongs to the reign of Tiberius, as some think, then the plural form probably refers to Tiberius and his mother, Livia. [3]**Puteol**: abbrev. for **Puteolīs**. [3–4]**a · d · IV · Idus M[aias] pr · Id · Mai · et · XVII · XV · K · Iu[nias]**: abbrev. for **ante diem quārtum Īdūs Māiās, prīdiē Īdūs Māiās et diē septimō decimō, diē quīntō decimō ante Kalendās Iūniās.** [5]**erit**: seems to be an error for **erunt**, since the subject **vēla** is plural. [5]**Magus**: the name of the sign painter.

70. 7995; III, vi, 2; Via dell'Abbondanza.

1 **D · Lucreti · Satri**
2 **Valentis · flaminis · [[Neronis]] · Caesaris · Aug · f · perpetui · glad · par · XX · et**
3 **D · Lucreti · Valentis · fili [· glad] · par · X**
4 **ex · a · d · V · K · April · venatio · et · vela · er[unt]**

For the sponsor, see I, 2, 64 and I, 2, 67. [2]**[[Nerōnis]]**: see I, 2, 67, note 2. [2–3]: supply the verb **pugnābant** after the noun phrases **glad · par · XX** and ·

glad] · par · X. [4]**ex a d V K Aprīl**: abbrev. for **ex ante diem quīntum Kalendās Aprīlēs**. The object of **ex** is **ante diem quīntum Kalendās Aprīlēs**.

71. 9970; necropolis, Porta di Nocera; Via di Nocera.

glad · par · XX · A · Suetti
[. .]tenionis [e]t Nigri · liberti · pugna
Puteol · XVI · XV · XIV · XIII · Kal · Ap · venatio · et
athletae [· vela ·] erunt

Notice for gladiatorial contests to be held at Puteoli. The dipinto can not be accurately dated, but probably belongs to the period before AD 62. [2]**[. .]tenionis**: the editor suggests restoring **An]teniōnis** but this name does not exist. [2]**pugnā**: abbrev. for **pugnābunt**. [3]**XVI · XV · XIV · XIII · Kal · Ap**: abbrev. for **diē sextō decimō, diē quīntō decimō, diē quārtō decimō, diē tertiō decimō ante Kalendās Aprīlēs**.

72. 9979; necropolis, Porta di Nocera; Via di Nocera.

ven · et · glad · par · XX
M · Tulli · pugn · Pom · pr · Non · Novembres
VII · Idus · Nov

The year of the contests cannot be determined. [1]**vēn**: abbreviation for **vēnātiō**. Supply the verb **erit** or understand **vēnātiō** in the sense 'troop of beast fighters.' [2]**Pom**: abbreviation for **Pompeīs**. [2]**pr Nōn Novembrēs, VII Īdūs Novembrēs**: to judge from the following inscription, which refers to the same contests, the syntax for the dates must be **ex prīdiē Nōnās Novembrēs ad diem septimum Īdūs Novembrēs**.

73. 9980; necropolis, Porta di Nocera; Via di Nocera.

venat · et · glad · par · XX · M · Tulli
pug · Pom · pr · Non · Non · VIII · VII · Idu
Novembr

For the sponsor, see I, 1, 72. [1]**vēnāt**: abbreviation for **vēnātiō**. **pr · Non · Non · VIII · VII · Idu Novembr**: abbrev. for **prīdiē Nōnās Novembrēs, Nōnīs Novembribus, diē octāvō, diē septimō ante Īdūs Novembrēs**.

3. Gladiatorial Dipinti

74. 538; VII, v, 14–15; Vico dei Soprastanti.

1 **Tetraites · Prudes · Prudes · l · XIIX · Tetraites · l · [-]**
2 **abiat Venere Bompeiiana iratam qui hoc laesaerit**

Line 1 is painted above pictures of gladiators. In the first picture two gladiators are about to begin combat. The second picture shows the two competitors near the end of the fight. Line 2 is painted at the bottom margin of the picture. This line scans as an iambic senarius. [1]**Tetraites**: note the mention in Petronius (*Satyricon*, 52; 71) of a famous gladiator by the name of **Petraites**. [1]**Prūdēs**: §2.1 **ns**, cf. **Prūdēns**. [1]**l**: abbrev. for **līber**. [1]**XIIX**: supply **pugnārum**. The final letter of this line, which indicated the number of fights by **Tetraites**, is illegible. [2]**abiat**: §2.1 **h** and §2.1 Hiatus, cf. **habeat**. [2]**Venere Bompeiiana**: acc. sg. fem. §2.1 Word-final Consonants: **m**. The writing of **b** for **p** in **Bompeiiana** is unusual. Note also the spelling of intervocalic [yy] by means of double **ii** rather than the customary spelling with single **i**, cf. **Pompeiāna**. [2]**laesaerit**: fut. perf. of **laedō**. Note that **ae** spells short **e** in the future perfect suffix **-eri-**, cf. **laeserit**.

75. 1111; II, vi; Amphitheatre.

1 **omnia munera vicisti**
2 **ton he<p>ta theamaton esti**

Painted near drawing of a gladiator. [1]**omnia mūnera**: acc. of specification. [1]**mūnera**: 'gladiatorial combats.' [2]This line is Greek although it is written in the Latin alphabet. Translate: 'He is one of the seven wonders of the world.'

76. 1182; necropolis, Porta di Nocera; Via di Nocera.

1	**munere [N Fes]ti Ampliati · d[i]e · summo ·**	
2	**Bebryx · Iul · XV · v**	**Nobilior · Iul · XIV**
3	**[– – –] · Iul · XVI ·**	**[– – –] Iu[l] m <Θ>**
4	**[– – –] Iul · XXX · v**	**[– – –]sus · Iul · XV · m · Θ**
5	**Hippolytus · [X]V · v ·**	**Ce[r]atus · Iul · VI ·**
6	**[Nedy]mus · Iul · V**	**[– – –]p[– – –] · Iul · XV · m ·**
7	**[– – –] Iul · IV [– – –]**	

Lines 2–7 are painted on top of pictures of six pairs of gladiators. Two additional pairs, the fifth one (two retiarii) and the eighth one (a Thracian and a Samnite), have no inscription. This dipinto was probably modelled on programs (**libellī**) announcing the pairings for gladiatorial combats. [2–7]: **Iul**: abbreviation for **Iūliānus**, the name of a gladiatorial school founded by Julius Caesar at Capua. [2]**Bebryx**: painted over two horsemen (**equitēs**). [2]**v**: abbrev. for **vīcit** 'was victorious.' [3]**m**: abbrev. for **missus est** 'was dismissed.' [3]Painted over a Thracian and a Samnite. The names of the gladiators are lost. [3]**<Θ>**: the inscription has an **e**. This symbol is an abbreviation for the Greek word ἀπέθανε, 'he died.' [4]Painted over a Thracian and a Samnite. The names of the gladiators are lost. [4]**Θ**: for the meaning of the symbol, see note 3. [5]Painted over two **secūtōrēs**. [6]Painted over a Thracian and a Samnite. The names of the gladiators are lost. [7]Painted over a Thracian and a Samnite. The names of the gladiators are lost.

4. Advertisements for Rentals and Sales

77. 138; VI, vi, 19; Via Consolare.

insula Arriana
Polliana [C]n Al[le]i Nigidi Mai
locantur ex [K] Iulis primis tabernae
cum pergulis suis et c[e]nacula
equestria et domus conductor
convenito Primum [C]n Al[le]i
Nigidi Mai ser

This inscription has 3 syntactic units: (1) lines 1-2; (2) lines 3-5, ending at **domus**; and (3) lines 5-7, beginning at **conductor**. [1]**Īnsula Arriāna Polliāna**: a city block named after **Arrius Pollio** and owned by **Gnaeus Alleius Nigidius Maius**. For **Nigidius Maius**, see I, 1, 20 and I, 2, 58 and I, 2, 66. [3]**locantur**: the subjects are **tabernae**, **c[ē]nācula** and **domus**. [3]**[K] Iūlīs prīmīs**: abbrev. for **Kalendīs Iūlīs prīmīs**. [5]**equestria**: 'fit for members of the equestrian class.' [5]**conductor**: refers to a person who rents an apartment, house, etc. 'a lessee.' [6]**convenītō**: 3rd sg. fut. impv. [7]**ser**: abbrev. for **servum**, in apposition to **Prīmum** (line 6).

78. 806/807; VIII, i, 44–45; Vico del Lupanare.

Sittius res
tituit

3 **elepan**
4 **tu**
5 **hospitium · hic · locatur**
6 **triclinium · cum · tribus · lectis**
7 **e[t] · comm**

This inscription has two syntactic units: (1) lines 1-4; (2) lines 5-7. The inscription accompanies a painting of a pygmy and an elephant. [1]**Sittius**: probably the name of the fellow who restored (**restituit**) the painting. [3-4]**elepantu**: acc. sg. masc., §2.1 Word-final **m**. [5]**hospitium**: 'lodgings.' [6]**comm**: abbrev. for **commodīs**, 'conveniences,' abl. pl. neut. [6]**trīclīnium**: in apposition to **hospitium**.

79. 1136; II, iv, 6; Via dell'Abbondanza.

1 **in · praedis · Iuliae · Sp · f · Felicis**
2 **locantur**
3 **balneum · Venerium · et · nongentum · tabernae · pergulae**
4 **cenacula · ex · Idibus · Aug · primis · in · Idus · Aug · sextas · anno[s · co]ntinuo[s · qu]inque**
5 **s · q · d · l · e · n · c**

[1]**praedīs**: abl. pl. of **praedium**, 'property.' Note that the abl. pl. ending and the stem-final **i** contract to **ī**. See §2.1 Contraction. [1]**Sp**: abbrev. for **Spurī**, praenomen of **Spurius**, gen. sg. masc. [1]**f**: an abbreviation for **fīliae**, gen. sg. fem. [1]**Iūliae · Sp · f · Fēlīcis**: the owner's name is **Iūlia Fēlīx**, daughter of **Spurius**. [2]**locantur**: the subjects are **balneum · Venerium · et · nongentum**, **tabernae**, **pergulae**, and **cēnācula**. [3]**Venerium**: this is an adjective, nom. sg. neut., meaning 'of Venus.' [3]**nōngentum**: gen. pl., 'the 900 hundred,' referring to officials who are in charge of ballot-vessels at elections. Presumably, this means that the bath is fit for the finest class of people. [4]**Aug**: abbrev. for **Augustīs**. [5]**s · q · d · l · e · n · c**: what this abbreviation stands for is uncertain. In my opinion, the most plausible interpretation is the following: **sī quis dēsīderābit locātrīcem eō nōmine conventīō**, 'If anyone will desire (to rent this property), let him/her meet the lessor for that purpose.' An alternative is: **sī quīnquennium dēcurrerit locātiō estō nūdō cōnsēnsū**, 'If the five-year lease period has expired, rent shall be by oral agreement.'

80. 7124; III, vii, 1; Via dell'Abbondanza.

tegula cumular
opercula colliquia
ven
convenito indide

Advertisement for sale of material salvaged from houses damaged by the earthquake of A.D. 62. [1]**tēgula**: acc. pl. neut., 'roofing.' [1]**cumulār**: abbrev. for **cumulāria**. [2]**opercula**: 'panels for walls,' acc. pl. neut. [2]**colliquia**: 'gutters' or 'drains.' [3]**vēn**: abbrev. for **vēnālia**, acc. pl. neut. of **vēnālis**, **-e**. This word modifies the nouns in lines 1–2. [4]The final portion of the dipinto appears to be incomplete. We expect the name of the seller or his representative. [4]**convenītō**: 2nd sg. fut. impv. [4]**indide**: adv. §2.1 Word-final Consonants: **m**.

5. Lost and Found

81. 64, add. pg. 191; VIII, iv, 33–34; Via dei Teatri.

urna aenia pereit · de · taberna
seiquis · rettulerit dabuntur
H–S LXV · sei · furem
dabit · unde · [rem]
servare po[ssimus H–S]
XX C IIII

Notice of theft of bronze pot from taberna. This inscription belongs to the oldest layer of wall inscriptions at Pompeii, dating to the Republican period. It is written in charcoal. [1]**aēnia**: 'made of bronze,' nom. sg. fem., cf. **aēnea**. In Pompeiian Latin short **e** in hiatus is often written as **i**. See §2.1 Hiatus. [1]**pereit**: This verb shows contraction of the verb stem **-i** and the 3rd sg. perf. ending **-it**. The letters **ei** commonly spell a long **ī** (see line 2, **sei** = **sī**). This verb is commonly spelled **periit**, but the contracted form **perīt** is not unusual. For contraction of **ii** and **iī**, see §2.1 Contraction. [2]**seiquis**: the letters **ei** represent a long **ī** (= **sī quis**). [2]**rettulerit**: the direct object is the bronze urn. [3]**H–S**: abbrev. for **sestertī**, nom. pl. masc. [3]**sei**: = **sī**. [4]**unde**: the adverb introduces a relative clause whose antecedent is **fūrem**. [4]**[rem]**: refers to the bronze urn. [5–6]**[H–S] XX C IIII**: supply **dabuntur**.

82. 3864; necropolis, Porta di Nocera; Via di Nocera.

1 **equa · {e}siquei · aberavit · cum · semuncis · honerata a d · VII · K[a]l {S[ept]embres} Decembres**
2 **convenito · Q · Deciu · Q · l · Hilarum · [au]t L [Deci]um · L l [Amp]hionem · citra pontem ·**
3 **Sarni ·**
4 **fundo ·**
5 **Mamiano ·**

Notice advertising the finding of a pack-horse. [1]**equa**: §2.1 Word-final Consonants: **m**. [1]**{e}sīquei**: the **e** at the beginning of this word is an error. Final **ei** represents long **ī** = **sīquī**; cf. §2.1 Long Vowels. For interrogative-indefinite **quī**, see I, 1, 31. **aberāvit**: note the single spelling of double **rr**. This verb, which is usually intransitive, is transitive here. [1]**cum**: followed by an instrumental ablative. [1]**sēmuncīs**: perhaps with the meaning, 'saddle-bags.' [1]**honerāta**: §2.1 Word-final Consonants: **m**. Word-initial **h** is added by hypercorrection. §2.1 Word-Initial **h**. **honerāta** modifies **equa**. [1]**Decembrēs** is written above **S[ept]embrēs** as a correction. [2]**Deciu**: §2.1 Word-final Consonants: **m**. [2]**l**: abbrev. for **lībertum**. [3]**Sarnī**: 'Sarno river,' gen. sg. masc. [5]**Mamiānō**: adj., 'belonging to Mamius,' the name of influential Pompeian family.

6. Public Acclamations and Salutations

83. 1074, add. pg. 199, pg. 461; IX, vii, 13; Via dell'Abbondanza.

1 **iudiciis · Augusti · Augustae feliciter**
2 **vobis · salvis · felices · sumus**
3 **perpetuo**

This inscription may refer to Nero's decision in AD 62 to permit the staging of gladiatorial combats in the amphitheatre. The games were suspended after the riot in AD 59. [1]**iūdiciīs**: 'decisions.' Note that **-iī** is not contracted. [1]**Augustī · Augustae**: refers to Nero and his wife, **Poppaea Sabīna**. [2]**vōbīs salvīs**: ablative absolute with conditional force.

84. 1084; VIII, vii, 20; large theatre.

1 **Satrio · Lucretio · Valenti · munifico**

2 **IV · sibi · liberis · feliciter · pro · Valente · ex · rog**

Acclamation in support of **Decimus Lucrētius Satrius Valēns**. See I, 2, 64, I, 2, 67, and I, 2, 70 for **Valēns** as the sponsor of gladiatorial games. [1]**mūnificō**: 'dutiful, fulfilling one's obligations,' here with reference to the financial backing of gladiatorial games. [2]**IV**: abbrev. for adv. **quater**. **ex · rog**: abbrev. for **exrogante**, 'who makes private expenditures,' abl. sg. masc. Note that the prefix is separated from its base by means of a punct.

85. 1085; VIII, vii, 20; large theatre.

1 **Paris**
2 **isse**
3 **val ·**

[1]**Paris**: this is the name of a famous pantomime. See also II, 5, 84, II, 5, 85, and II, 5, 89. [2]**isse**: assimilation of **ps** to **ss**, cf. **ipse**. The pronoun **isse** here indicates eminence. Translated as 'the great one.' [3]**val**: abbrev. for **valē**.

86. 1094; VIII, vii, 20; large theatre.

1 **Popidio · Rufo · invicto · muner ter**
2 **defensoribus · colon<o>rum · feliciter**

Numerius Popidius Rufus was a candidate for the duumvirate in the last 10 years of the city. For Rufus as sponsor of gladiatorial contests, see I, 2, 59. [1]**mūner ter**: the reading is difficult. **mūner** is probably an abbreviation for **mūnerāriō**. [2]**colōn<ō>rum**: the letters in the middle of this word are written by means of a ligature which does not seem to include an **o**.

87. 2993y; add. pg. 462; VIII, iii, 3; Via Marina.

1 **Σατριω**
2 **Ουαλεντι**
3 **Ο[γ]ουστω**
4 **Νηρ φηλικιτ**

This dipinto is Latin, but it is written in the Greek alphabet. [3]Note the spelling of the word-initial diphthong in **Ο[γ]ουστω** as **o** instead of **au**.

[4]**Νηρ**: abbrev. for **Nerōnī**. [4]**φηλικιτ**: abbrev. for **fēlīciter**. Transcribe as: **Satriō Valentī Ogustō (= Augustō) Ner(ōnī) fēlīcit(er).**

88. 3525; VI, xv, 1; Vicolo dei Vettii.

1 **iudicis · Aug · felic · Puteolos · Antium · Tegeano · Pompeios · hae · sunt · verae**
2 **colonia[e]**

The acclamation is in support of the decision of Nero to rescind the ban on gladiatorial contests. Compare I, 5, 83 and I, 5, 89. [1]**iūdicīs**: dat. sg. neut., §2.1 Contraction. Governed by **fēlīc(iter)**. [1]**Puteōlōs · Antium · Tegeāno · Pompeiōs**: for accusative case see §2.4 Accusatives in lists. The fact that Nuceria is not included in this list no doubt has to do with lingering animosity over the riot in AD 59. [1]**Tegeāno**: acc. sg. neut., cf. **Tegiānum**. See §2.1 Hiatus and §2.1 Word-final Consonants: **m**. The spelling of the accusative with **o** instead of **u** is not unusual at Pompeii.

89. 3726; IX, vi, b–c; street between IX, vi and IX, vii.

iudicis · Augusti · p · p · et · Poppaeae · Aug · feliciter

For the sentiment, compare I, 5, 83 and I, 5, 88. **iūdicīs**: dat. sg. neut., §2.1 Contraction. Governed by **fēlīciter**. **p · p**: abbrev. for **patris patriae**. **Poppaeae**: wife of Nero. **Aug**: abbrev. for **Augustae**.

90. 7687; II, v, 1; Via del'Abbondanza.

1 **ordini [fe]liciter**
2 **M · S · l · r · b · m · LX**
3 **[rog]amus**

Acclamation for the town council. [2]**M · S · l · r · b · m**: how the abbreviations are to be restored is open to conjecture. One suggestion is: **Mārcō Satriō līberīs reīpūblicae bene merentibus**. Supply **fēlīciter** to govern these datives. [3]**LX**: what the numerals refer to is not clear. [3]**rogāmus**: supply the name **Mārcum Satrium** as object.

91. 7755; III, vi, 2; Via dell'Abbondanza.

1 **Poliaeus Aug · cubiclarius · Marsus · hic · et · ubique sa[lutem]**
2 **[sa]n[cti]issimae · coloniae · et · populo · Pompei<a>no ubique sal**

Acclamation in support of the colony and of people of Pompeii. [1]**Aug**: abbrev. for **Augustī**. [1]**cubiclārius**: §2.1 Syncope. [1]**sa[lūtem]**: supply the verb **dīcit**. [2]**sal**: abbrev. for **salūtem**. Supply the verb **dīcit**. The subject of both verbs is **Poliaeus Marsus**.

92. 7990; II, vii; Palestra.

1 **Cn · Alleio · Maio**
2 **principi · munerarior**
3 **feliciter**

Acclamation in support of **Māius** as sponsor of gladiatorial games. For **Māius**, see I, 2, 58 and I, 2, 66. [2]**mūnerāriōr**: abbrev. for **mūnerāriōrum**.

93. 9888; II, vi, 3; Via dell'Abbondanza.

1 **Satrio**
2 **feliciter**
3 **Iustae · feliciter**
4 **Valentinae · feliciter**
5 **D · L · V · [f]**
6 **feliciter**

Acclamation for **Satrius** and family. See I, 5, 84 and I, 5, 87. [1]**Satriō**: for **Satrius** as sponsor of gladiatorial contests, see I, 2, 64 and I, 2, 67. [3]**Iūstae**: wife of **Satrius**. [4]**Valentīnae**: probably the daughter of **Satrius**. [5]**D · L · V · [f]**: abbreviation for **Deciō Lucrētiō Valentis fīliō**.

7. Miscellaneous Dipinti

94. 89, add. pg. 192; Via dei Sepolcri.

Glyco cum Martial[e]
sole [ca]llente sities h[ac]

sitiēs: §2.1 **ns**, cf. **sitiēns**. **sole [ca]llente**: ablative absolute. **h[ac]**: adv., 'here.'

95. 294; VII, iii, 14; Via della Fortuna.

Iuen
illa nata
di{i}e Satu
ora secu
v IIII Non Au

Birth announcement. The name **Iuenilla** is painted around the picture of an infant. [1-2]**Iuenilla**: **u** stands here for [uw], cf. **Iuvenilla**. [3]**di{i}ē**: misspelling for **diē**. [3]**Sātu**: abbrev. for **Sāturnī**. [4]**ōrā**: §2.1 **h**, cf. **hōra**. [4]**secu**: abbrev. for **secundā**. [5]**v**: abbrev. for **vespertīnā**. **Au**: abbrev. for **Augustās**.

96. 813; VII, xi, 13–14; Vicolo del Lupanare.

otiosis · locus · hic non est discede
morator

Painted next to a gigantic snake. This dipinto scans as a dactylic hexameter if the **i** of **ōtiōsīs** is treated as a semivowel **y**. There are two syntactic units, the first of which ends at **est** in line 1. [2]**morātor**: voc. sg. masc.

97. 882; IX, iii, 1–10; Via Stabiana.

Pilo[ca]lus * votum * sol * libes * merito

Near a painting of the goddess Isis Panthea. The graffito is in the form of a votive text. *: the punctuation is in the shape of leaf. **sol**: abbrev. for **solvit**. **libēs**: §2.1 **ns**.

98. 1096, add. pg. 202; II, vi; amphitheatre.

permissu
aedilium · Cn ·
Aninius · Fortu
natus · occup ·

[1]**permissū**: with the permission of the aediles vendors set up stalls for sale of food and drink in the arches beneath the amphitheatre. [4]**occup**: abbrev. for **occupāvit**.

99. 1096a, add. pg. 202; II, vi; amphitheatre.

[per]missum aedil
occupavit

[1]**[per]missūm**: abl. sg. masc. = **permissū**. Final **m** is added by hypercorrection. §2.1 Word-final Consonants: **m**. [1]**aedīl**: abbrev. for **aedīlium**.

100. 1173, add. pg. 204; location unknown.

quisquis ·
ama valia
peria · qui · n
osci · amare
bis [t]anti pe
ria quisqu
is · ama[re]
vota

This dipinto is in the form of an elegiac couplet. Lines 1–4 form the first metrical unit; lines 5–8 make up the second. After line 8, there are eight additional lines, but they are difficult to read and impossible to interpret. For another version of the same couplet see II, 7, 121. [2–8]**ama**, **valia**, **peria** (2x), **nosci**, and **vota**: 3rd sg. forms with loss of **t**, §2.1 Word-final Consonants: **t**. [2]**valia**: §2.1 Hiatus. [3]**peria**: §2.1 Hiatus. [3–4]**nosci**: this probably spells the verb phrase **nōn scit**. Note that the sequence **ns** is regularly spelled as **s**, cf.

§2.1 **ns**. [5]**tantī**: genitive of value. [5]**bis [t]antī**: the usual construction is **bis tantō**, ablative of degree of difference; cf. II, 7, 129. [8]**vota**: = **vetat**., cf. **vetet**, II, 7, 129.

101. 2953; VII, ii, 18; Vico del Panattiere.

C · Vivi
Itale
frunis ·
carus · s · Ati
a tua

[1–2]**C · Vivī Itale**: voc. sg. masc., **Gāius Vivius Italus**. [1]**C**: abbrev. of **Gāī**, vocative singular of **Gāius**. [1]**Vivī**: probably a spelling of the voc. sg. of the family name **Vibius**. For some Pompeiians medial **b** was pronounced with a sound close to **v** in Latin, perhaps similar to the intial sound in English *vain*. This sound was spelled by **v**. §2.1 **b** and **v**. [3–4]**frūnis · cārus**: despite the word divider, the best guess here is that this is a single word, namely, the 2nd sg. pres. subj. of the deponent verb **frūniscor** 'enjoy.' This verb is found in Old Latin in Plautus and Cato, and in imperial Latin in Petronius, but is not found in authors of the classical period. The verb takes accusative case in these authors, but ablative is attested in inscriptions of the imperial period. [4]**s**: what this letter stands for is uncertain. [4–5]**Atia tua**: acc. sg. fem. or abl. sg. fem., object of **frūniscārus**.

102. 2960; IX, ?, ?; Vico di Balbo.

o [T]ite aegrotes

A curse. **aegrōtēs**: for the form compare I, 1, 41.

103. 2993b; VIII, iii, 3 (?); Via Stabiana.

Secundus
Primae sue

[2]**suē**: dat. sg. fem., cf. **suae**. §2.1 Monophthongization. [2]Supply the verb phrase **salūtem dīcit**.

104. 2993c; VIII, iii, 3; Via Stabiana.

Secundus
Prime ·
[suae] sal

[2]**Prīmē**: §2.1 Monophthongization. [3]**sal**: supply the verb **dīcit**.

105. 3494i; VI, xiv, 36; Via dei Vettii.

itis ·
foras ·
rixsatis

Painted next to a picture in which the tavern-keeper is pushing outside two men who are quarreling. [1–3]**ītis, rixsātis**: 2nd pl. indicative but with the function of imperatives. Supply **et** to conjoin the two verb phrases. [2]**forās**: adv. with verbs expressing motion, 'out of doors.' [3]**rixsātis**: cf. deponent (**rixor, rixārī**). Occasionally the digraph **xs** spells the consonant cluster **ks**. The reason seems to be the feeling that two consonants should be spelled by two letters.

106. 3779; IX, vii, 21; Vicolo di Tesmo.

Hospitium
C Hugini Firmi

Painted on exterior wall. [2]**Hugīnī**: note the spelling **u** for Greek **y**.

107. 3832; IX, xiii, 1; Via dell' Abbondanza.

cacator
cave · malu

This dipinto was found in a room next to a latrine. It was placed next to the painting of a man defecating between two serpents. [2]**malu**: §2.1 Word-final Consonants: **m**.

108. 3877; necropolis, Via di Nocera.

scaen[ae] domine
v[a]le

The dipinto may refer to the pantomine, Paris. See II, 5, 83 and II, 5, 84.

109. 6641; V, 6, 18; Via del Vesuvio.

cacator · sig · valeas ·
ut · tu · hoc · locum trasea

This dipinto was found near the water reservoir located just south of Porta Vesuvio and as such serves as a warning against defecating near the water supply. See III, 1, 1 and note also I, 7, 111. [1]**sig**: change of **c** to **g** before voiced **v** of **valeās**; see §2.1 Word-final Consonants: **t**. [2]**locum**: neuter gender here. **trāseā**: abbrev. for **trāseās**; cf. **trānseās**. §2.1 **ns**. The final **s** is omitted because of a nail.

110. 7037; V, iv, Vicolo di M. Lucretius Fronto.

Circinaeus · hic · habitat

111. 7038; V, iv, Vicolo di M. Lucretius Fronto.

stercorari
ad murum
progredere · si ·
presus fueris · poena ·
patiare necese
est · cave

Warning against dumping dung in the city. Compare III, 1, 1. The graffito has three parts: (1) lines 1–3, **stercorārī** to **prōgredere**; (2) lines 3–6, **sī** to **est**; (3) **cavē**. [1]**stercorārī**: voc. sg. masc. [2]**ad mūrum**: the wall that surrounds the city of Pompeii. [3]**prōgredere**: 2nd sg. dep. impv. [4]**prēsus**: past participle of **pre(he)ndō**, cf. **prēnsus**. §2.1 **ns**. [4]**prēsus fueris**: 2nd sg. fut. perf. pass., cf. **prēnsus eris**. [4]**poena**: §2.1 Word-final Consonants: **m**. [5]**patiāre**: 1st. conj. act.

inf. The verb is deponent in Classical Latin, but active forms appear in Old Latin writers, e.g., **patiās**, Naevius, *Com.* 67. [5]**necese**: the geminate **s** of **necesse** is spelled with a single **s**.

112. 7350; I, x, 4; Via del Tempio d' Iside.

Menander –
hic primus
omn[iu]m com
ediam scripsit

This dipinto is incised next to a picture of the Greek new comedy poet Menander. Three lines are painted beneath this dipinto but they are difficult to interpret and may not be connected to the text presented here. [3–4]**cōmēdiam**: the usual spelling is **cōmoedia**.

113. 7716; III, v, 1; Via dell' Abbondanza.

cacator · cave malum
aut · si · contempseris · habeas
Iove · iratum

See I, 7, 107. [2]**aut**: 'or else.' [2]**contempseris**: as direct object supply **hoc**, 'this (warning).' [3]**Iove**: acc. sg. masc., §2.1 Word-final Consonants: **m**.

114. 9839b; I, xii, 1–2; Via di Nola.

abomino paupero
quisqui quid gratis
rogat fatus est
aes · det et ac
cipiat rem

This inscription has three parts: (1) line 1; (2) lines 2–3; (3) lines 4–5. [1]**abominō**: in literary Latin this verb is usually deponent. [1]**pauperō**: acc. pl. masc. with second declension inflection, rather than third. For second declension forms compare **pauperōrum**, gen. pl. masc., Petronius, *Satyricon*, 46.1. For loss of final **s** see §2.1 Word-final Consonants: **s**. [2]**quisqui**: loss of final **s**. §2.1 Word-final Consonants: **s**. [3]**fatus**: loss of **u** before **u**, cf. **fatuus**. [5]**rem**: here with the meaning 'product.'

II. GRAFFITI FROM POMPEII

1. Salutations and Wishes

1. 1227, add. pg. 205, add. pg. 463, add. pg. 704; VI, i, 7; Via Consolare.

1 **venimus**
2 **huc cupidi**
3 **multo**
4 **magis**
5 **hire · ut**
6 **liceat**
7 **nostros**
8 **visere**
9 **Roma Lares**

A graffito written by a visitor to Pompeii. This inscription has 2 syntactic units: (1) lines 1–2; (2) lines 3–9. [1]**vēnimus**: perf. act. [3–9]Supply **cupīmus** (4th conjugation) as the main verb for the second sentence as per II, 7, 145 and *CIL* IV.2995 (**[vēnim]us hōc cupidī, multō magis īre cupīmus**). This verb governs the infinitive **hīre**. Note further that the placement of **cupīmus** after **hīre** permits the graffito to be scanned as an elegiac couplet. [3]**multō**: abl. of degree of difference. [5]**hīre**: word-initial **h** by hypercorrection, cf. **īre**. §2.1 Initial **h**. Translate 'go back, return.' [7–9]**nostrōs . . . Larēs**: acc. pl. masc., direct object of **vīsere**. [9]**Rōma**: voc. sg. fem.

2. 1241; VII, i, 16; Vico Narcisso.

1 **Secundus quoservis**
2 **proficisces salutem**
3 **libes**

[1]**quōservīs**: **qu** is a spelling for **c**, cf. **cōnservīs**. For long **ō** see §2.1 **ns**. [2]**proficīscēs**: §2.1 **ns**. [2]**salūtem**: supply **dīcit**. [3]**libēs**: §2.1 **ns**, cf. **libēns**.

3. 1347; ?, ?, ?; Via di Mercurio.

1 **felices homines va**

felices

[1]**fēlīcēs hominēs**: voc. masc. pl. **va**: abbreviation for **valēte** or **valeāte**. [2]**fēlīcēs**: repetition of line 1; supply **hominēs valēte** or **hominēs valeāte**.

4. 1512; VI, xiv, 38; Vico dei Vettii.

Nolanis - feliciter

Nōlānīs: the adjective is used substantively, 'the people of Nola.' The town of Nola is located approximately 20 miles east northeast of Pompeii. **fēlīciter**: adverb used elliptically with the meaning 'good luck.'

5. 1611; VII, iii, 38; Vicolo Storto.

Salinesibus · feliciter

Salinēsibus: §2.1 **ns**. The word refers to the people of a city district in Pompeii, 'the Salinienses.' The location of this neighborhood is near the Porta Ercolano. In I, 1, 4 the spelling is **Saliniēnsēs**. In **Salinēsibus i** has been elided in hiatus before **ē**.

6. 1852; VIII, i, 2; Basilica, Vicolo di Championnet.

Pyrrhus · Chio · conlegae · sal
moleste · fero · quod audivi ·
te · mortuom · itaq val

This graffito has three parts: (1) line 1; (2) lines 2–3, **molestē** to **mortuom**; (3) **itaq val**. [1]**Chiō**: dat. sg. masc. of **Chius**, a cognomen of Greek origin. [1]**conlēgae**: etymological spelling of **collēgae**. [1]**sal**: abbrev. for **salūtem**. Supply **dīcit** as verb. [2]**molestē ferō**: idiomatic expression, 'I am troubled.' [2]**quod**: causal conjunction. [3]**tē mortuom**: supply **esse** in indirect statement after **audīvī**. [3]**mortuom**: acc. sg. masc. In 2nd declension nouns and adjectives like **servus**, **mortuus**, and **equus** the letter **o** is occasionally written in the nominative and accusative singular instead of **u**. [3]**itaq**: abbrev. for **itaque**. [3]**val**: abbrev. for **valē**.

7. 1937; VIII, i, 2; Basilica, Via Marina.

1 **quisque me · ad c[e]nam**
2 **vocarit v**

[1]**quisque**: here used in the sense of **quisquis**. The use of **quisque** as an indefinite relative is as old as Plautus. [2]**vocārit**: 3rd sg. fut. perf., §2.3 Perfect Tense. [2]**v**: abbrev. for **valeat**.

8. 1983; VII, viii; Forum, Via Marina.

1 **have**
2 **L · Pop ·**

[1]**havē**: §2.1 Word-Initial **h**, cf. **avē**. [2]**L · Pop**: abbrev. for **Lūcī Popidī**, voc. sg. masc. of **Lūcius Popidius**.

9. 2018c; VII, xi, 11; Vico del Balcone Pensile.

mendax veraci ubique salute

mendāx and **vērācī** are used as substantives. **salūte**: §2.1 Word-final Consonants: **m**. Supply the verb **dīcit**.

10. 2059; VII, xiii, 3; Via dell'Abbondanza.

Ianuarias nobis felices multis annis

Iānuāriās . . . fēlīcēs: acc. of exclamation. **multīs annīs**: abl. of duration of time.

11. 2083, add. pg. 465; VII, i, 8; Via dell'Abbondanza.

Myrtile · habias · propitium Caesare

Myrtile: voc. sg. masc., cognomen of Greek origin. **habiās**: §2.1 Hiatus, cf. **habeās**. **propitium**: take as predicate adjective after **habiās**. **Caesare**: acc. sg. masc., §2.1 Word-final Consonants: **m**.

12. 2124; VII, i, 8; Via dell'Abbondanza.

Nero<n>i · Caesri · Agusto

Supply either the adverb **fēlīciter**, 'good luck,' or the verb phrase **salūtem dīcō**. **Nerō<n>ī**: the graffito reads **Nerōī**. **Caesrī**: medial **a** is lost by syncope, cf. **Caesarī**. See §2.1 Syncope. **Agustō**: perhaps an error for **Augustō**, but this could also be **Āgustō** since there is some evidence in Vulgar Latin for the change of **au** to **ā** when the following syllable contains the vowel **u**, e.g., **āscultāre** for **auscultāre**, 'listen to, pay attention to.'

13. 2152; VII, xii, 35; Vico di Eumachia.

coloniae · Clau
Neronesi · Putiolane
feliciter
scripsit · C · Iulius · Speratus
Sperate · va

This graffito has three syntactic units: (1) lines 1–3; (2) line 4; (3) line 5. Line 5 was added by another person. [1]**Clau**: abbreviation for **Claudiānae**, 'associated with the emperor Claudius.' [2]**Nerōnēsī**: §2.1 **ns**. [2]**Putiolānē**: dat. sg. fem., 'of Puteoli.' In addition to the monophthongization of final **ae**, note the change of **e** to **i** in hiatus, cf. **Puteolānae**. See §2.1 Monophthongization and §2.1 Hiatus. [5]**Spērāte**: voc. sg. masc. [5]**va**: abbrev. for **valē**.

14. 4007; I, iii, 30; Vicolo di Paquio Proculo (?).

Tu pupa sic valeas
sic habeas
Venere Pompeianam
propytia <

[1]**pupa**: voc. sg. fem. [3]**Venere**: acc. sg. fem., §2.1 Word-final Consonants: **m**. **propytia**: acc. sg. fem., §2.1 Word-final Consonants: **m**. In this word the letter **y** spells the short vowel **i**. [4]<: This sign appears to mark the end of the inscription. Two lines are incised beneath line 4 but they are gibberish.

15. 4100; V, ii, 4; Via di Nola.

fullo
Cresces
coponi sal

[2]**Crēscēs**: §2.1 **ns**. [3]**cōpōnī**: §2.1 Monophthongization. [3]**sal**: abbrev. for **salūtem**; supply the verb **dīcit**.

16. 4109; V, ii, 4; Via di Nola.

fullo ·
Cresces ·
Stabianis ·
salute

[2]**Crēscēs**: §2.1 **ns**, cf. **Crēscēns**. [4]**salūte**: §2.1 Word-final Consonants: **m**. Supply **dīcit**.

17. 4118; V, ii, 4; Via di Nola.

ulula est
Cresces · fullonibus · et · ululae · suae · sal

Line 1 appears to have been incised by a different person than line 2. [1]**Crēscēs**: §2.1 **ns**, cf. **Crēscēns**. [2]**sal**: abbrev. for **salūtem**; supply the verb **dīcit**.

18. 4477; VI, xiii, 19; Via del Labirinto.

Daphnicus cum Felicula sua hac
bene Felicule bene Daphnico
utriusque bene eveniat

[1]**hāc**: adv., 'here.' Supply the verb **fuit**. [2]**Fēlīculē**: dat. sg. fem. §2.1 Monophthongization. [3]**utrīusque**: gen. sg. The reason for the genitive, rather than dative, is not clear.

19. 4753; VII, vii, 5; Via Marina.

Aephebus –
Successo patri
suo salut

[1]**Aephēbus**: cognomen of Greek origin, cf. **Ephēbus**. **Ae** stands for short **e** here. §2.1 Monophthongization. [3]**salut**: abbrev. for **salūtem**. Supply the verb **dīcit**.

20. 4783; VII, vii, 5; Via Marina.

Cresces · have · anima
dulcis · et · suavis

[1]**Crēscēs**: voc. sg. masc., cf. **Crēscēns**. §2.1 **ns**. [2]**have**: **h** is written by hypercorrection, cf. **avē**. §2.1 **h**. [2]Supply the verb **es**.

21. 4811; VI, xiii, 19; Vico del Labirintho.

va Modesta va · valeas · ubicumq es

ubicumq: abbrev. for **ubicumque**.

22. 6700; V, iii, 9; Vico di M. L. Frontone.

Vesbine copo va

cōpō: voc. sg. masc., §2.1 Monophthongization, cf. **caupō**.

23. 6815; VI, vxi, 45; Via del Vesuvio.

felicem Aufidium Felicem semper deus
faciat

[2]**faciat**: subjunctive of wish.

24. 6867; villa rustica, Boscoreale.

Cerdo sodalibus
Brundisio

Supply **dīcit salūtem**. **Brundisiō**: §2.4 Ablative for Locative.

25. 8505; II, vii; Palaestra.

Priscus caelator
Campano
gemmario
fel

[1]**Priscus caelātor**: supply the verb **dīcit** and take **Priscus caelātor** as subject. [4]**fel**: abbrev. for **fēlīciter**. It governs the datives in lines 2–3.

26. 8657; II, vii; Palaestra.

ic sumus
felices
valiamus
recte

[1]**īc**: §2.1 **h**. [3]**valiāmus**: §2.1 Hiatus. [3–4]**valiāmus rēctē**: 'may we be in really good health.'

27. 8670; II, vii; Palestra.

ic abitamus
felices
nos
dii
faciant

This graffito has to parts: (1) line 1-2; (2) lines 2-5. **fēlīcēs** (line 2) is no doubt to be understood with both parts. [1]**īc abitāmus**: §2.1 **h**. [4]**diī**: nom. pl. masc. **diī** may be a misspelling for **dī** or **deī**, although it is possible that this form shows short **i** for **e** in hiatus, cf. **deī**. §2.1 Hiatus.

28. 8883; III, v, 2; Via dell' Abbondanza.

Terminalis sorori plurima salute

Written in charcoal. **plūrima salūte**: §2.1 Word-final Consonants: **m**. Supply **dīcit**.

29. 8903; III, v, 4; Via dell' Abbondanza.

Ga Sabinius · Statio · plurima · sal
viator · Pompeis pane gustas
Nuceriae bibes ·
Nucer[ia]e [– – –]

This graffito has to parts: (1) line 1; (2) lines 2-4. [1]**Gā**: abbrev. for **Gāvius**. [1]**plūrima**: acc. sg. fem., §2.1 Word-final Consonants: **m**. [2]**sal**: supply the verb **dīcit**. [2]**viātor**: voc. sg. masc. [2]**pane**: acc. sg. fem., §2.1 Word-final Consonants: **m**. [3]**bibes**: 2nd sg. pres. act., §2.1 Short **i**. Supply **vīnum** as direct object. [4]The end of this line is illegible, but it may be a repetition of the previous line, in which case read **Nucer[ia]e [bibes].**

30. 8954; III, vii, 2; Via dell' Abondanza.

Habitus
issae sal

[2]**issae**: the usual dative singular ending is **-ī**. Here **-ae** is by analogy with other **a**-declension endings in the paradigm; cf. **illae**, II, 7, 119. The meaning of **issae** in this graffito is similar to the meaning of **domina**, 'mistress.' [2]**sal**: supply the verb **dīcit**.

31. 9143; ins. occ., 19; Via Consolare.

P[o]mpeianis · ubique sal

sal: supply the verb **dīcō**.

32. 9171; necropolis, Porta Vesuvio; Via del Vesuvio.

sic [t]ib[i] contingat semper florere Sabina contingat
forma{e} sisque puella diu

This graffito refers to **Poppaea Sabīna**, a native of Pompeii who married the emperor Nero. See also I, 1, 14, I, 5, 80, and I, 6, 90. The graffito is an elegiac couplet. The pentameter begins at the second **contingat** and this word begins the second wish. [1]**contingat**: the infinitive **flōrēre** is the subject. [1]**Sabīna**: voc. sg. fem. [1]**contingat**: the subject is **fōrma{e}** in line 2. [2]**forma{e}**: error for **forma**.

2. Curses and Insults

33. 1662; VII, vii, 22 (?); Vico di Soprastanti.

Verus hic ubi stat
nihil veri

[1]After **Verus hīc** supply the verb **fuit**. [1]**stat**: the subject is **Verus**. [2]**nihil vērī**: supply the verb **est**.

34. 1816; VIII, i, 2; Basilica, Via Marina.

Epaphra · glaber · es

Epaphra: cognomen of Greek origin, voc. sg. masc.

35. 1839; VIII, i, 2; Basilica, Via Marina.

Agato Herenni serus rogat Venere
ut periat rogo

Line 2 is written by a different person. [1]**Agatō**: cognomen of Greek origin, nom. sg. masc. [1]**Herennī**: gentilicium, gen. sg. masc., cf. **Herennius**. For the spelling of the genitive singular of 2nd declension nouns in **-ius**, see §2.2 2nd Declension Genitive Singular. [1]**serus**: nom. sg. masc., cf. **servus**. Loss of **v** [w] before the back vowel **u**. [1]**Venere**: acc. sg. fem., §2.1 Word-final Consonants: **m**. [2]**periat**: §2.1 Hiatus, cf. **pereat**. Supply the noun **Agatō** from line 1 as subject of **periat**.

36. 1864; VIII, i, 2; Basilica, Via Marina.

Samius
Cornelio
suspendre

A curse. [1–2]Supply the verb **dīcit** after **Cornēliō**. [3]**suspendre**: loss of medial **e** by syncope, cf. **suspendere**. §2.1 Syncope. **suspendre** is best interpreted as an infinitive with imperative function. The meaning is reflexive, 'go hang yourself.'

37. 1949; VIII, i, 2; Basilica, Via di Marina.

Oppi · emboliari · fur · furuncule

All of the words are in the vocative case. **emboliārī**: refers to a type of entertainer who performs skits at interludes between theatrical performances. Perhaps best translated here as 'clown, buffoon' since the context is derogatory.

38. 2082; VII, i, 8; Via dell' Abbondanza.

in cruce
figarus

[Facsimile 13] A curse. [2]**fīgārus**: 2nd sg. pass. subj. of **fīgō**, **fīgere**, 'fasten up, fix, nail.' The ending **-rus** is to be set beside the usual deponent/passive endings **-ris** and **-re**. See §2.3 2nd Singular Deponent/Passive.

39. 2409a; VII, i, 1; Via dell' Abbondanza.

Stronius
Stronnius
nil scit

This graffito seems to have been written by different people. Line 1 may have been written by **Stronius** himself. Later, another writer added lines 2 and 3 as a derogatory comment and misspelled the name **Stronius**!

40. 3948; I, ii, 24; Vicolo del Conciapelle.

talia te fallant
utinam medacia copo
tu vedes acuam et
bibes ipse merum

This graffito, which is an imprecation against an innkeeper, is in the form of an elegiac couplet. [1–2]The subject of **fallant** is **tālia . . . medācia**. [2]**medācia**: loss of **n** before **d**, cf. **mendācia**. §2.1 Nasal + Stop Consonant. [2]**cōpō**: voc. sg. masc., §2.1 Monophthongization. [3]**vedes**: loss of **n** before **d**, cf. **vendis**. See §2.1 Nasal + Stop Consonant and §2.1 Short **i**. **vedes** must scan as a spondee, even though the final syllable is metrically light. [3]**acuam**: trisyllabic and scans as an anapest. Compare *aquae* at Lucretius 6, 552, which also scans as trisyllabic. The final syllable of **acuam** does not elide before the vowel of **et**. [4]**bibes**: §2.1 Short **i** , cf. **bibis**.

41. 4430; VI, vii, 1; Vicolo della Fullonica]

Glove dicet Sympore
vale Naev[os] male periat
opordet

This graffito has two parts: (1) lines 1–2, **Glovē** to **valē**, which is a greeting to **Sympora**; (2) lines 2–3, **Naev[os]** to **opordet**, an imprecation. [1]**Glovē**: nom. sg. fem. of **Chloē**, a cognomen of Greek origin. Note the spelling of **chl** as **gl** and the writing of the transitional semivowel **v** between **o** and **ē**. The noun maintains Greek inflexion. [1]**dīcet**: 3rd sg. pres. act., §2.1 Short **i**. [1]**Symporē**: dat. sg. fem. of **Symphora**, a cognomen of Greek origin. §2.1 Monophthongization. [2]**periat**: §2.1 Hiatus. [3]**opordet**: medial **t** is changed to **d**, cf. **oportet**. Voicing of medial voiceless stops is infrequently attested at Pompeii. **opordet** governs the subjunctive **periat** in line 2.

42. 4764; VII, vii, 5; Via Marina.

Perari –
fur – es

[1]**Perārī**: voc. sg. masc.

43. 4765; VII, vii, 5; Via Marina.

Aephebe –
ardalio – es

[1]**Aephēbe**: cognomen of Greek origin, voc. sg. masc., cf. **Ephēbos**. Note the spelling of word-initial **e** by **ae**. See I, 1, 19 and §2.1 Monophthongization. [2]**ardaliō**: probably a misspelling for **ardeliō**.

44. 4833; VII, xv, 8; Vicolo del Gallo.

Nype Crispini ancla necuisma

Nypē: nom. sg. fem. with Greek inflection, cf. **Nymphē**. For loss of **m** before **p**, see §2.1 Nasal + Stop Consonant. **ancla**: probably a misspelling for **ancilla**. **necuisma**: §2.1 Syncope, cf. **nequissima**. Supply the verb **est**. Note also that the labiovelar [k^w] is spelled by **cu**.

45. 4993; IX, ii, 18; Vico di Tesmo.

Ampliatus Pedania fur [est]

After **Ampliatus** supply **dīcit**. The final portion of the graffito is difficult to read.

46. 5279; IX, viii, 2; Via di Nola.

tu · mortus · es ·
tu · nugas · es

[1]**mortus**: nom. sg. masc. Loss of **u** before a back vowel, cf. **mortuus**. [2]**nugās**: probably nom. sg. masc. with assimilation of **x** (= **ks**) to **ss** and then simplification of **ss** to **s** in final position.

47. 6701; V, iii, 9; Vicolo di Lucretius Fronto.

fur {v} cave
siq

[1]{v}: an error. [1]**cavē**: supply the word **malum**, cf. II, 2, 49. [2]**siq**: this may be an abbreviation but of what is not clear.

48. 6864; IX, v, 11; Via di Nola.

optume maxime
Iupiter domus omnipotes
Acratus servo nequa

Lines 1–2 form the first sentence, line 3 forms the second. [1-2]**optume maxime Iūpiter**: voc. sg. masc. [2]**domus**: probably a syncopated form of **dominus**, *viz.*, **domnus** (for which see *CIL* IV.4356), with **n** accidentally omitted, §2.1 Syncope. Note that **domus** is nominative case in apposition to vocatives. [Another possibility here, though less likely in my opinion, is that **domūs** is gen. sg. fem., 'home,' in which case supply 'protector' *vel sim.* to govern this genitive.] [2]**omnipotēs**: voc. sg. masc., §2.1 **ns**. [3]**servo**: nom. sg. masc. In 2nd declension nouns and adjectives like **servus**, **mortuus**, and **equus** the letter **o** is occasionally written in the nominative and accusative singular instead of **u**. For loss of word-final **s**, see §2.1 Word-final Consonants: **s**. [3]**nēqua**: indecl. adj., nom. sg. masc., cf. **nēquam**. Supply the verb **est**.

49. 8645; II, near Amphitheatre.

Mus cave
malum

[1]**Mus**: voc. sg. masc.

50. 10070; II, iii, 10; ?.

Lesbiane cacas scribis que [sa]lute

que: note that the enclitic is written as a separate word. **[sal]ūte**: §2.1 Word-final Consonants: **m**. Supply **tibi dīcō**.

51. 10119; II, vii; Palaestra.

Lite es · dipundi
Lite

aeris a

[1]**Lite**: voc. sg. masc. [1]**dipundī**: gen. of value. [3]**a**: abbrev. for **assis**, gen. sg. masc. [3]**aeris a**: gen. of value. Supply the verb **es**.

52. 10243; necropolis, Porta di Nocera; Via di Nocera.

Macer cerebri moti

Macer: voc. sg. **cerebrī mōtī**: gen. of quality. Supply **vir es** *vel sim*.

53. 10243h; necropolis, Porta di Nocera; Via di Nocera.

C Raro male eveniat

C: abbrev. for **Gāiō**.

3. Gladiators

54. 1293; VI, ix, 6–7; Via di Mercurio.

Campani victoria una
cum Nucerinis peristis

Incised beneath a drawing of a gladiator and gladiatorial equipment. This graffito refers to the riot that broke out between spectators in the amphitheatre at Pompeii in AD 59. The riot left some Nucerians injured and others dead. The Roman Senate held an investigation and ordered the amphitheatre closed for ten years. For an account see Tacitus, *Annales* XIV.17. [1]**Campānī**: voc. pl. masc. This may refer to members of a fan club that supported gladiators. **victōriā**: abl. of means. **ūnā**: adv. Construe with the prep. **cum**. [2]**perīstis**: §2.1 Contraction, cf. **periistis**.

55. 1329; ?, ?, ?; Via di Mercurio.

Nucerinis
infelicia

For context, see note to II, 3, 54. **īnfēlīcia**: acc. of exclamation.

56. 1421, add. pg. 461; VI, xi, 10; Vicolo di Mercurio.

1	**Faustus Itaci Neronianus ad amphithiatru[m]**	
2	**[P]riscus · N ·**	**H[er]ennius**
3	**VI · v**	**[l XIIX p]**

Inscribed above drawings of gladiators. [1]**Itaci**: probably an error for **Iatacus**. See II, 3, 73. Supply **servus** to govern the genitive. [1]**amphithiātru[m]**: note **i** for **e** in hiatus, cf. **amphitheātrum**. §2.1 Hiatus. [1]Supply the verb **pugnāvit**. [2]**N**: abbrev. for **Nerōniānus**, referring to a gladiatorial school started by Nero. [3]After the numerals, which refer to the number of fights, supply **pugnārum**. [3]**v**: abbrev. for **vīcit**. [3]**l**: abbrev. for **līber**. [3]**p**: abbrev. for **periīt**.

57. 1422; VI, xi, 10; Vicolo di Mercurio.

1	**Asteropaeus**	**Ocea{nea}nus**
2	**Ner CVII**	**l VI**
3	**v**	**m**

Inscribed above drawings of two gladiators. [1]**Ōcea{nea}nus**: an error for **Ōceanus**. [2]**Ner**: abbrev. for **Nerōniānus,** referring to name of gladiatorial school. [2]After the numbers understand **pugnārum**. [3]**m**: abbrev. for **missus est**.

58. 1474; VI, xii, 2; Via della Fortuna.

1	**Spiculus · Ner v**	**Aptonetus p**
2	**tiro**	**libr · XVI**

Incised above a drawing of two gladiators. On the left, a gladiator is poised for attack. The gladiator on the right has been felled and is sprawled on the ground. [1]**Ner**: abbreviation for **Nerōniānus**, referring to the name of a gladiatorial school. [2]**tīrō**: this term refers to a recently recruited gladiator. [2]**lībr**: abbreviation for **līber**. [2]XVI: supply **pugnārum**.

59. 1653; VII, 6, 29 (?); Vico dei Soprastanti.

Hermaiscus invictus hac

Inscribed above a drawing of a gladiator. **invictus**: 'undefeated' in gladiatorial combats. **hāc**: perhaps with the meaning of **hāctenus**, 'so far.'

60. 1989; VIII, 3, 24 or 2, 14; Strada delle Scuole.

heic · venatio · pugnabet · V · K · Septembres
et · Felix · ad · ursos · pugnabet

[Facsimile 14] This graffito is in the style of an **ēdictum mūneris**. [1]**heic**: **ei** spells **ī**. §2.1 Long Vowels. **vēnātiō pugnābet**: the best interpretation is that **vēnātiō** is used concretely to mean 'troop of animal hunters.' [1]**pugnābet**: §2.1 Short **i**. [1]**V · K**: abbrev. for **quīntō diē ante Kalendās**. [2]**ad**: for **adversus** in the sense of 'against.'

61. 2183; VII, xii, 18; Vico del Lupanare.

Puteolanis feliciter
omnibus Nucherinis
felicia et uncu · Pompeianis
Petecusanis

For the context, see II, 3, 53. This graffito was composed by two writers. Lines 1 and 2, and the first word of line 3, were written by one scriptor. Line 3, beginning with **et**, and line 4 were written by a different scriptor. [2]**Nucherīnīs**: **ch** is a common spelling for χ in loanwords from Greek, and this spelling is occasionally extended to non-Greek words, as here. [3]**uncu**: §2.1 Word-final Consonants: **m**. [3]**fēlīcia** and **uncu** are accusatives of exclamation. [4]**Petēcūsānīs**: note **e** for **i** in the first syllable and the spelling of original aspirated **th** as **t**, cf. **Pithēcūsānīs**. The reason for **e** rather than **i** in the first syllable is perhaps due to the **ē** in the following syllable.

62. 2398, add. pg. 221; IX, i, 22; Via dell' Abbondanza.

proeliare Gangens Caesar te spectat

proeliāre: 2nd sg. dep. impv. **Gangēns**: voc. sg. masc. **n** is written by hypercorrection, cf. **Gangēs**. §2.1 **ns**.

63. 2437, add. pg. 466; VII, vii, 16; portico between theatres.

C · Ae[l]lius · Astraga[l]us
curator
fuit · IV · Non · Dec · usce ad ·
VI · Eid Dec · M · Agrip T Stat · cos
ce[t]uria C · Iuli · Heleni · turma
C · Iuli · Hilari

This graffito is dated to AD 37. [2]**cūrātor**: here referring to the sponsor of gladiatorial games. [3]**usce**: the letter **c** probably spells [k^{W}] here, cf. **usque**. [4]**Agrip**: abbrev. for **Agrippā**, abl. sg. masc. [4]**Stat**: abbrev. for **Statiō**, abl. sg. masc. [4]**cos**: abbrev. for **cōnsulibus**. This noun phrase forms an ablative absolute. [5]**ce[t]uria**: **n** is lost before **t**, cf. **centuria**, 'troop of gladiators.' §2.1 Nasal + Stop Consonant. [5]**turma**: 'troop of mounted gladiators.'

64. 2483, add. pg.466; VIII, vii, ludus gladiatorius; Via Stabiana.

Manuetus provocator
victor Veneri par
mam feret

[1]**prōvocātor**: this type of gladiator wore a heavily folded loincloth with a broad metal belt; a greave to above the knee on the left leg; an arm-guard on the right arm (**manica**); and a helmet with a large horizontal neck-guard, cheek-guards, and ornamentation on the front. The **prōvocātor** carried a shield (**parma**) and a short sword with a straight blade.

65. 4280; V, v, 3; Via di Nola.

esse
Philippus Tettia VIII c VIII

[1]**esse**: abbrev. for **essedārius**. There are no pictorial depictions of this type of gladiator so we have no information about equipment or manner of fighting. [2]**Tettiā**: abbrev. for **Tettiānus**, which probably refers to a gladiatorial school. [2]**VIII**: supply **pugnārum**. [2]**c**: abbrev. for **corōnārum**, 'victory crowns.' These were awarded for success in especially noteworthy gladiatorial contests. [2]The last half of line two should read: **pugnārum VIII corōnārum VIII**.

66. 4289; V, v, 3; Via di Nola.

1 **puelarum**
2 **decus Celadus**

[1]**puelārum**: double consonants are occasionally represented by a single letter.

67. 4297; V, v, 3; Via di Nola.

Celadus Oct III c · III

Oct: abbrev. for **Octāviānus**. III c · III: supply **pugnārum** and read **pugnārum III corōnārum III**.

68. 4299; V, v, 3; Via di Nola.

1 **V K Aug Nuceriae Florus vic**
2 **XIIX K Sept Herclanio vicit**

[Facsimile 15] [1]**vic**: abbrev. for **vīcit**. [2]**Herclāniō**: §2.4 Ablative for Locative. See also §2.1 Syncope and §2.1 Hiatus, cf. **Herculāneum**.

69. 4302; V, v, 3; Via di Nola.

1 **Rusticus Malius XII c XI**
2 **M · Terntius III c III**

Following these two lines are three lines that are very difficult to read. [2]**Terntius**: abbrev. for **Terentius**. Spellings such as this one, in which the letter **n** represents the syllable **en**, reflect what is called 'syllabic notation' or 'abbreviated spelling.'

70. 4342; V, v, 3; Via di Nola.

1 **suspirium puellarum**
2 **Tr**
3 **Celadus · Oct III · c III**

[1]**suspīrium puellārum**: this noun phrase is in apposition to **Tr Celādus Oct**. [2]**Tr**: abbrev. for **Thraex**. This term refers to a type of gladiator known as 'Thracian.' The **Thraex** wore a pair of very high greaves reaching to the knees; above the knees there was ribbed padding up to the hips. On his right arm he wore an arm-guard (**manica**), and on his head a helmet with a crescent-shaped crest and a griffin's head. He carried a small round shield (**parmula**) and a short curved sword (**sīca**). [3]**Oct**: abbrev. for **Octāviānus**.

71. 4345; V, v, 3; Via di Nola.

1 **puellarum decus**
2 **Celadus Tr**

72. 4356; V, v, 3; Via di Nola.

1 **Tr**
2 **Celadus reti**
3 **Cresces**
4 **pupar{r}u domnus I**

[2]**rēti**: abbrev. for **rētiārius**. The **rētiārius** fought with a throwing net (**iaculum**), which he held in his right hand, and a trident (**fuscīna** or **tridēns**) or long dagger in his left. He was naked except for a loincloth and a tall shoulder-guard on his left shoulder (**galerus**). [3]**Crēsces**: §2.1 **ns**, cf. **Crēscēns**. [4]**pupar{r}u**: gen pl. fem., cf. **pupārum**; §2.1 Word-final Consonants: **m**. The geminate spelling of **r** is an error. [2]**domnus**: §2.1 Syncope, cf. **dominus**. [4]**I**: supply **pugnae** or **corōnae**.

73. 4795; VII, viii; Forum, Via Marina.

Iatacus cum Nicephoro lus

Inscribed next to the figure of gladiator. **lūs**: abbrev. for **lūsit**. Here perhaps with the meaning 'to play for stakes, to gamble.'

74. 4870; VIII, ii, 20; Via delle Scuole.

1 **Q · Ptronius · m**
2 **Otaus XXXIIII v**
3 **Severus · v**

4 **lib XXXXXV**

Lines 3–5 are incised to the right of lines 1–2. [1]**Ptrōnius**: abbrev. for **Petrōnius**. The letter **p** represents the syllable **pe**. This is another example of 'syllabic notation,' cf. II, 3, 69. [2]**Otāus**: simplification of **ct** to **t**, cf. **Octāvus**. The letter **u** probably stands here for **vu**. [2–4]Understand **pugnārum** as partitive genitive after the numerals.

75. 8056; I, vi, 15; Via del Tempio d' Iside.

Severu[s] l XIII · Albanus · sc · l · XIX v

[Facsimile 16] This graffito is incised next to the figures of two gladiators. The figure of **Severus** has dropped his shield on the ground in front of him. **Albānus** holds his sword in his left hand. **l**: abbrev. for **līber**. **sc**: abbrev. for **scaeva**, 'left-hander.'

76. 10236; necropolis, Porta di Nocera; Via di Nocera.

1	**M Att**	
2	**M · Attilius I c I**	**L Raecius Felix**
3	**v**	**XII c XII · m**

This graffito is incised next to the figures of two gladiators. The figure of **Raecius Fēlīx** is on his knees, his helmet on the ground in front of him.

77. 10238; necropolis, Porta di Nocera; Via di Nocera.

1	**M Attilius t v**	**Hilarus Ner XIV c XIII**
2	**v**	**m**

[Facsimile 17] This graffito is incised next to the figures of two gladiators in combat. **t**: abbrev. for **tīrō**, 'novice.'

4. Soldiers

78. 1711; VII, i, 41; Via degli Augustale.

M · Nonius · Campanus · mil · coh · VIIII · pr · c · Caesi

mīl: abbrev. for **mīles**. **coh**: abbrev. for **cohortis**, gen. sg. fem. **pr**: abbrev. of **praetōriae**. **c**: abbrev. of **centuriae**. **Caesī**: the genitive means that Nonius was a member of the century of Caesius.

79. 1994; VIII, iii, 21; Via delle Scuole.

Sex · Decimius · Rufus
milis · coh · V pr · c · Martialis

[2]**mīlis**: nom. sg. masc., §2.1 Short **i**. **Martiālis**: gen. sg. See I, 4, 78.

80. 2157; VII, xii, 35; Vico di Eumachia.

C · Valirius · Maximus
milis domus

[1]**Valirius**: note the spelling of **i** for **e**, cf. **Valerius**. [2]**mīlis**: nom. sg. masc., §2.1 Short **i**.

81. 3992; I, iii, 3; Via dell' Abbondanza.

Q Spurennius Priscus
primpilar
pilar

[2]**prīmpilār**: abbrev. for **prīmipilāris**. The term refers to the centurion who commands the first century of the first cohort of a legion. [3]**pilār**: abbrev. for **pilārius**, 'juggler'? It seems likely that **pilār** in line 3 was added for comic effect by a second hand.

82. 8405; I, x, 11; Vico di Tesmo.

C · Anneus
Capito
eq · coh · X · pr
c · Grati

[1]**Anneus**: §2.1 Monophthongization, cf. **Annaeus**. [3]**eq**: abbrev. for **eques**.

5. Entertainers

83. 1294; VI, ix, 6; Via di Mercurio.

calos Paris isse
Septentrio

[1]**calōs**: either the Greek adverb, καλῶς, 'hurrah!,' or possibly the adjective, καλός. [1]**Paris**: for the actor see I, 6, 85. [1]**isse**: assimilation of **ps** to **ss**, cf. **ipse**. The pronoun is used here to indicate eminence. Translate as 'the great one.' [2]**Septentriō**: supply **scrībit**.

84. 1305; VI, ix, 5; Via di Mercurio.

Paris · hic
fuit

85. 3891; I, ii, 6; Via Stabiana.

Acti · Anicete · va
Hore · va

[1]**Āctī · Anicēte**: voc. sg. masc., name of a popular actor. See below II, 5, 87 and 88. [2]**Hōre**: voc. sg. masc., name of an actor.

86. 4767; VII, vii, 5; Via Marina.

Fumiolus
cum archimimo
a sipario
Receptus

This graffito has two parts: (1) lines 1-2; (2) lines 3-4. [1-2]**Fūmiolus**: supply the verb phrase 'was here.' [3]**sīpariō**: small curtain concealing part of the stage and used as backdrop for performances by mimes. [4]**Receptus**: supply **scrībit** or **scrīpsit**.

87. 5395; necropolis, Porta di Nocera; Via di Nocera.

Acti · a[mor]
populi cito
redi va

[1]**Āctī**: voc. sg. masc. [1]**a[mor]**: governs the genitive **populi**. [2]**cito**: take this adverb with **redī** in line 3.

88. 5399; necropolis, Porta di Nocera; Via di Nocera.

Acti dominus
scaenicorum va

[1]**Āctī**: voc. sg. masc. [1]**dominus**: nominative in apposition to a vocative.

89. 8888a; III, v, 3; Via dell' Abbondanza.

Triaria Paridianis sal

Paridiānīs: refers to the troop of the pantomime Paris. **sal**: supply **dīcit**.

6. Lists, Memoranda, Notices

90. 1392; VI, xi, 16; Via del Labirinto.

III · Idus · Apriles
tunica · I *

[2]**tunica**: acc. sg. fem. §2.1 Word-final Consonants: **m**. For the accusative, see §2.4 Accusative in Lists. [2]*****: symbol for **dēnāriō** abl. sg. masc. Abl. of price.

91. 1393; VI, xi, 16; Via del Labirinto.

K XII · Maias · tun · pal
Nonis Mais fas ·
VIII · Idus · Mas
tunicas · II

[1]**K XII**: the order should be **XII K**. [1]**tun**: abbrev. for **tunicam**. [1]**pal**: abbrev. for **pallium**. [2]**fas**: abbrev. for **fasciam**. [3]**Mas**: abbrev. or error for **Māiās**. For the accusatives, see §2.4 Accusatives in Lists.

92. 1679, add. pg. 210; VII, ii, 45; Via degli Augustali.

invicte Castresis
habeas · propiteos
deos · tuos · tres it
e et qui leges
calos Edone
valeat · qui legerit
Edone · dicit
assibus · hic
bibitur · dipundium
si dederis meliora
bibes quattus
si dederis vina · {f}
Falerna bib calos{c} Castresi<s>

This inscription is best divided into four parts: (1) Lines 1–4 are a benediction to a mimic actor named **Castrēnsis**. (2) Lines 5–6 form a salutation to **Ēdonē**. (3) Lines 7–13 up to **bib** is an advertisement for a taberna. (4) The end of line 13 seems to repeat the benediction for **Castrēnsis**. [1]**Castrēsis**: §2.1 **ns**. [2]**propiteōs**: note the spelling of original **i** by **e**, cf. **propitiōs**. §2.1 Hiatus. [3]**deōs · tuōs · trēs**: this probably refers to the tutelary triad of the city of Pompeii, *viz.*, Hercules, Bacchus, and Venus. [3–4]**ite**: §2.1 Word-final Consonants: **m**, cf. **item**. [4]**et quī leges**: this is addressed to the person who reads the inscription. [5]**calōs**: the Greek adverb καλῶς, 'hurrah!' [5]**Ēdonē**: cognomen with Greek inflexion, nom. sg. fem., cf. **Hēdonē**. Loss of initial **h**, §2.1 **h**. The word means 'delight.' [6]**quī lēgerit**: take the subject of **valeat** as the antecedent of the relative. [7]**Ēdonē dīcit**: Edone's speech has three parts: (1) **assibus - bibitur**; (2) **dīpundium - bibēs**; (3) **quattus - bib**. [9]**bibitur**: impersonal passive, 'one drinks.' [9]**dipundium**: 'the sum of two *asses*.' The usual form of this word is **dupondius**, but **dipondius**, **dupundius**, and **dipundius**, which is the form found here, are also attested. [10]**meliōra**: supply **vīna**. [11]**quattus**: indecl. masc., 'the sum of four asses.' [12]**{f}**: error for **Falerna**, line 13. [13]**Falerna**: 'Falernian.' The adjective refers to a district in northern Campania that was famous for the quality of its wines. [13]**bib**: abbrev. for **bibēs**. [13]**calōsc**: the Greek adverb καλῶς; word-final **c** was probably written erroneously in anticipation of the initial **C** of **Castrēsi<s>**.

[13]**Castrēsi<s>**: §2.1 **ns**. Final **s** is probably omitted by error. Supply the verb **valeās**?

93. 1754, add. pg. 211, add. pg. 790; Porta Marina, Via di Marina.

Eupemus
stecus · e fundo · et
rota

Notice of items for sale. [1]**Eupēmus**: cognomen of Greek origin, cf. **Euphēmus**. [2]**stecus**: perhaps an error for **stercus**, but this could also be a case of the simplification of the cluster **rc** to **c**. Note **stecora**, nom. pl. neut, IV, 2, 9. [3]**rota**: §2.1 Word-final Consonants: **m**.

94. 2070; VIII, iv, 4; Via dell' Abbondanza.

IIX · Id Iulias axungia p · CC
aliu · manuplos CCL

List of supplies incised on a column in the peristyle. [1]**Īd**: abbrev. for **Īdūs**. [1]**axungia**: §2.1 Word-final Consonants: **m**. §2.4 Accusative in lists, etc. This word generally refers to axle-grease, but that seems out of place here. Perhaps it simply means 'lard.' [1]**p**: abbrev. for **pondō**. [1]**CC**: supply **lībrārum**, 'pounds.' [2]**āliu**: §2.1 Word-Final Consonants: **m**. §2.4 Accusative in Lists. [2]**manuplōs**: note the syncope of medial **u** between **p** and **l**, §2.1 Syncope. Note also that **u** rather than **i** is written before medial **p**. See §2.1 Short **i** and **u** in Medial Syllables and compare **manipulōs**. [1–2]**axungia p · CC, aliu · manuplōs**: the relationship between **auxungia** and **p · CC** and between **aliu** and **manuplōs CCL** is appositional rather than dependent.

95. 2464; VIII, vi, Ludus Gladiatorius; Via Stabiana.

VII K · Febr
tabulas · positas
in · muscario
CCC VIIII

[1]**Febr**: abbrev. for **Februāriās**. [2]**tabulās positās**: see §2.4 Accusative in lists. [3]**muscāriō**: a 'safe' to protect writing tablets from flies. [4]**CCCVIIII**: the number of writing tablets. Earlier editions of this inscription indicate that there may have been additional numbers.

96. 4000; I, iii, 27; Vicolo di Tesmo.

oleum l a IV
palea a V
faenum a XVI
diaria a V
furfure a VI
viria I a [–]
oleum a VI

List of ingredients and supplies incised on wall of a bakery. All forms are accusative as per §2.4 Accusative in Lists. [1]**l**: abbrev. for **lībram**, 'a pound.' **a**: abbrev. for **assibus**. [2]**palea**: acc. sg. fem., 'corn husks.' §2.1 Word-final Consonants: **m**. [4]**diāria**: acc. pl. neut. of **diārium**, 'daily ration of food' (for prisoners, slaves). [5]**furfure**: 'bran.' §2.1 Word-final Consonants: **m**. **viria**: acc. sg. fem., 'bracelet.' §2.1 Word-final Consonants: **m**.

97. 4182; V, ii, i; Via delle Nozze d' Argento.

Nerone Caesare Augusto
Cosso Lentulo Cossi fil cos
VIII Idus Febrarias
dies Solis luna XIIIIX nun Cumis V nun Pompeis

Notice for market-day. The date is February 6, AD 60, but this was not a Sunday, and the full moon fell on February 5. [2]**fīl**: abbreviation for **fīliō**, abl. sg. masc. [3]**Febrāriās**: note the loss of **u** after **br** in this word. **lūnā**: abl. of separation. [4]**XIIIIX**: supply **diēs**. [4]**nun**: abbrev. for **nundinae**. [4]**V**: supply **Idūs Febrāriās**.

98. 4495; VI, xiii, 19; Vicolo dei Labirinto.

a d XI K Iun
[D] A[cc]ius auctio
nem fecit et eo
VI N VIII
VI K Iun m

Notice concerning an auction. [1]**a d XI K Iūn**: abbrev. for **ante diem XI Kalendās Iūniās**. [2]**[D] A[cc]ius**: this is conjecture. The name cannot be restored with accuracy. [3]**eō**: adv., 'in addition.' [4–5]**VI N VIII VI K Iūn**: additional dates on which the auction was held. Abbrev. for **VI Nōnās, VIII Kalendās Iūniās, VI Kalendās Iūniās**. [5]**m**: what is intended by this character is not clear. It may stand for an abbreviation, but for what?

99. 4528; VI, xiv, 28; Via del Vesuvio.

IV Idus Feb Vettia
*** XX – usu a – XII**
Non Febra Faustilla
*** XV usu a VIIII**

[1]**Feb**: abbrev. for **Februāriās**. [2]*****: symbol for **dēnāriōs**. [2]**ūsū**: abbrev. for **ūsūra**. [2]**a**: abbrev. for **assēs**. [3]**Nōn Febra**: abbrev. for **Nōnīs Februāriīs**. [3]**Febra**: there is space between the letters **r** and **a**, but there does not appear to be a letter missing. There are other examples of this word in which **u** has been lost after the consonant cluster **br**, cf. II, 6, 97. [4]**ūsū**: abbrev. for **ūsūra**. [4]**a**: abbrev. for **assēs**.

100. 4811; VII, xv, 3; Vicolo del Gallo.

trici · modius XXX
modios
amphras [.] V

Inventory of amount of wheat and number of amphoras. [1]**trici**: gen. sg. neut., cf. **triticium**. Note syncope of medial **i** and assimilation of **tc** to **c(c)**. For syncope compare **frīdam**, II, 9, 161. [1]**modius**: corrected to **modiōs** in line 2. [2]**modiōs**: §2.4 Accusative in lists, etc. [3]**amphrās**: syncope of medial **o**, §2.1 Syncope. §2.4 Accusative in Lists. [3]**[.] V**: the first number is illegible.

101. 5181; IX, vi, 8; Vico del Centenario.

VII K Dec Salinis in conventu
multa HSS XX

[1]**Salīnīs**: abl. pl. fem. of **Salīnae**, name of Pompeiian district. The word has locative function. For additional references to this district, see I, 1, 4 and II, 1,

5. [2]**multa**: 'money from fines.' [2]**HSS**: abbrev. for **sēstertī**, nom. pl. masc. Supply the verb **numerābantur**, *vel sim.*

102. 5432; villa rustica, Boscoreale.

VII Idus · Maias
auct · fact
Germanico · cos

This graffito is dated to AD 12. Notice of an auction. [2]**auct**: abbrev. for **auctiō**. [2]**fact**: abbrev. for **facta**. Supply **est**. [3]**Germānicō**: Germanicus Julius Caesar, son of the emperor Tiberius. [3]**cos**: abbrev. for **cōnsule**.

103. 6733; V, iv, 1; Via di Nola.

ex XIIII K Apriles diaria reliquimus

relīquimus: here in the sense of 'fail' or 'neglect to give.'

104. 6853; VI, xvi, 29; Vico dei Vettii.

XVI K Feb coco venit

coco: nom. sg. masc., cf. **cocus** and **coquus**. §2.1 Word-final Consonants: **s**. It is possible that the writer intended **cōpō** instead of **coco**, but the third letter, at least to judge by the drawing of the graffito in *CIL* IV, appears to be **c**.

105. 6877; Villa Rustica, Boscoreale.

operaris pane denariu

operārīs: §2.2 1st and 2nd Declension Dative/Ablative Plural. **pane**: §2.1 Word-final Consonants: **m**. §2.4 Accusative in Lists. **dēnāriu**: §2.1 Word-final Consonants: **m**. Accusative of price, 'for a denarius.' This function is usually carried by ablative case.

106. 6886; Villa Rustica, Civita Giuliana.

palos · acutos DCCCXL

qui non · acuti CDLX
summa MCCC

Inventory of wooden posts. [1]**pālōs**: §2.4 Accusative in lists, etc. [2]**quī**: supply **pālōs** as antecedent. [3]**summa**: §2.1 Word-final Consonants: **m**.

107. 6887; villa rustica, Civita Giuliana.

in acervo MXXIII
magno
pali sunt

Inventory of wooden posts. [1]**MXXIII**: the number is to be taken with **pālī sunt**.

108. 8203; I, viii, 13; Via di Castricio.

Idibus Iulis
inaures postas ad Faustilla
pro * II usura deduxit aeris a
ex sum XXX

[Facsimile 18] This inscription is divided into two parts: (1) lines 1–2; (2) lines 3–4. [2]**inaurēs**: acc. pl. fem., 'earrings.' §2.4 Accusative in Lists. [2]**postās**: cf. **positās**, §2.1 Syncope. Translate as 'deposited.' [3]**Faustilla**: §2.1 Word-final Consonants: **m**. [3]**prō**: §2.4 Prepositions. This preposition governs * = **dēnāriō** and II (**assibus**). [3]*****: abbrev. for **dēnāriō**. [3]**II**: supply **assibus**. [3]**ūsūra**: §2.1 Word-final Consonants: **m**. [3]**a**: abbrev. for **assem**. [3]**dēdūxit**: 'subtracted' from an amount. [4]**ex sum**: abbrev. for **ex summā**. [4]**XXX**: = **tricē(n)simam**, in agreement with **ūsūra**.

109. 8489; II, v, 3; Via dell'Abbondanza.

oliva · condita
XVII · K · Novembres

[1]**olīva condita**: probably acc. sg. fem., §2.4 Accusative in Lists. §2.1 Word-final Consonants: **m**. [1]**condita**: 'bottled.'

110. 8938; III, vii, 1; Via dell'Abbondanza.

Duaci <c>apela Donat<a> nomine aberaut

Notice of loss of a she-goat. **Duācī**: gen. sg. masc., a name referring to the owner of the **<c>apela**. **<c>apela**: initial **c** is erroneously omitted. The word is spelled here with one **l**, but the usual spelling is **capella**. **Dōnāt<a>**: erroneous omission of final **a**. **aberaut**: 3rd sg. perf., cf. **aberrāvit**. Once again, note the spelling of the double consonant (**rr**) by a single letter, and note also the loss of **i** in the final syllable. For discussion of perfects with syncopated ending **-aut**, see §2.1 Syncope.

111. 8972; XIV, iv, 4; Via di Nola.

XIII · K · Maias · panem · feci

112. 9109; IX, xii, 2; Via dell' Abbondanza.

scripsi · coeptum stamin{i}
Decembre VII K Ianuarias

[1]**coēptum**: supply est. [1]**stāmin{i}**: probably a nom. sg. neut. with **i** for **e**. The word-final **{i}** is an error. See §2.1 Short **i**.

113. 9997; I, ix, 5; Via del Tempio d' Iside.

solitas emi as I
VIII Idus Dec
cera I s

Written in charcoal. [1]**solitās**: supply **cērās** in the sense of 'writing tablets coated with wax.' [1]**as**: abbrev. for **asse**. [3]**cēra**: §2.1 Word-final Consonants: **m**. Supply the verb **ēmī**. **s**: abbrev. for **sēmisse**.

7. Love and Lust

114. 1222; Porta di Ercolano.

amamus

2 **invidemus**

115. 1454, add. pg. 196, 207; VI, vi, 1; Via delle Terme.

1 **hic · habitat**
2 **felicitas**

This inscription is incised in stone. It is inscribed above and below a phallic symbol.

116. 1645; VII, vi, 35; Vico dei Soprastanti.

1 **si · quis forte · meam · cupiet · vio[lare]**
2 **puellam · illum · in · desertis**
3 **montibus · urat · amor**

The graffito is in the form of an elegiac couplet. The first metrical unit ends with the word **puellam**, line 2.

117. 1649; VII, vi, 35; Vico dei Soprastanti.

1 **alliget · hic · auras · si · quis**
2 **obiurgat · amantes · et · vetet**
3 **assiduas · currere · fontis**
4 **aquas**

The graffito is in the form of an elegiac couplet. The dactylic hexameter ends with **amantēs**, line 2. [1]**hic**: must scan as heavy. It refers to **quis**, subject of the conditional clause. [1]**quis**: this word must scan as heavy. [2]**et**: the conjunction links the parts of the apodosis, **alliget · hic · aurās** and **vetet assiduās** . . . . [2]**vetet**: takes accusative + infinitive, 'to prevent' accusative 'from' infinitive.

118. 1665; VII, vi, 25; Vico dei Soprastanti.

1 **Restituta · cum Secundo**
2 **domno suo**

[1]Supply the verb phrase **fuit hīc**. [2]**domnō**: §2.1 Syncope, cf. **dominō**.

119. 1824, add. pg. 464, pg. 704; VIII, i, 2; Basilica, Via Marina.

quisquis amat veniat Veneri volo frangere costas
fustibus et lumbos debilitare deae
si potest illa mihi tenerum pertundere pectus
quit ego non possim caput i[ll]ae frangere fuste

Lines 1–2 form an elegiac couplet; lines 3–4 are in dactylic hexameter. [1]**volo**: the 1st singular ending is short by iambic shortening. [1]**frangere**: **fr** does not make position. [3]**potest**: the final syllable scans as light, perhaps by loss of **t** in **st** cluster, cf. **pos** = **post**, **es** = **est**. [3]**illa**: refers back to **deae**, **Venerī**. [3]**mihi**: scan as an iamb. [4]The apodosis of the conditional sentence is in the form of a deliberative question, which is the reason for subjunctive **possim**. [4]**quit**: inter. adv., 'why,' cf. **quid**. The spelling of original **d** by **t** must be by hypercorrection. See §2.1 Word-final Consonants: **t**. Metrically, this word scans as a heavy syllable. [4]**i[ll]ae**: dat. sg. fem. The usual form is **illī**. Here the **-ae** is due to analogy with other **a**-declension forms in the paradigm; cf. **issae**, II, 2, 30.

120. 1898; VIII, i, 2; Basilica, Via Marina.

quisquis amat calidis non debet fontibus uti
nam · nemo · flammas · ustus · amare potest

This graffito is in the form of an elegiac couplet. [1]**fontibus**: 'springs; baths.'

121. 1928, add. pg. 465, pg. 704; VIII, i, 2; Basilica, Via Marina.

scribenti · mi · dictat · amor · mostratque · cupido
ad peream · sine · te · si · deus esse velim

This graffito is in the form of an elegiac couplet. [1]**mī**: dat. sg. of **ego**. [1]**mōstratque**: cf. **mōnstrat**, §2.1 **ns**. [2]**ad**: §2.1 Word-final Consonants: **t**, cf. **at**. [2]**sine**: this is the first word of the protasis of the conditional sentence.

122. 1948, add. pg. 213; VIII, i, 2; Basilica, Via Marina.

Lucilla ex corpore lucrum faciebat

ex corpore: abl. of means expressed by prepositional phrase.

123. 2060; VII, xiii, 3; Via dell' Abbondanza.

1 **Romula**
2 **hic · cum**
3 **Staphylo**
4 **moratur**

124. 2146; VII, xii, 35; Vicolo di Eumachia.

1 **Vibius Restitutus hic**
2 **solus · dormivit et Urbanam**
3 **suam desiderabat**

125. 2310b; VII, ii, 21; Vico di Panattiere.

1 **Euplia hic**
2 **cum hominibus · bellis**
3 **m m**

[1]**Euplia**: the name of a prostitute. [3]**m m**: abbrev. for **duōbus millibus**.

126. 2413h; IX, vii, 16–17 (?); Vicolo di Tesmo.

1 **Cestilia regina Pompeianoru**
2 **anima dulcis va**

[1]**Pompēiānōru**: §2.1 Word-final Consonants: **m**.

127. 2414; VIII, vii, 16; portico between theatres.

1 **propero · vale · mea · Sava ·**
2 **fac · me · ames ·**

This graffito has three syntactic units: (1) line 1, **properō**; (2) line 1, **valē** to **Sava**; (3) line 2. [1]**Sava**: cognomen. [2]**fac · mē · amēs**: note lack of subordinating conjunction **ut**.

128. 2457; VIII, vii, 16; portico between theatres.

1 **Methe Cominaes Atellana amat Chrestum · corde [si]t utreis**
2 **que Venus Pompeiana · propitia [e]t sem[per] concordes · veivant**

This graffito has two syntactic units: (1) line 1, **Mēthē** to **Chrestum**; (2) lines 1–2, **corde** to **veivant**. [1]**Methē**: cognomen of Greek origin, cf. **Menthē**. §2.1 Nasal + Stop Consonant. [1]**Cominiaes**: gentilicium, gen. sg. fem., §2.2 1st Declension Genitive Singular. Supply **ancilla** to govern the genitive. [1]**Atellāna**: 'from (the town of) Atella.' [1–2]**utreis que**: in the plural = **ambō**. The letters **ei** spell long **ī**. §2.1 Long Vowels. Note that the pronominal form is spelled as two words. [3]**veivant**: §2.1 Long Vowels.

129. 4091; V, i, 23–26; Via Stabiana.

1 **quis amat valeat pereat qui**
2 **nescit amare bis tanto pereat**
3 **quisquis amare vetat**

This graffito is in the form on an elegaic couplet. The pentameter begins at **bis**, line 2. In order for the hexameter to scan properly, read **quisquis** for **quis** at the beginning of line 1. Compare inscription I, 7, 101.

130. 4498; VI, xiii, 19; Via del Labirinto.

1 **Thyas x**
2 **noli · amare**
3 **Fortunatu**
4 **vale**

[1]**Thyas**: cognomen of Greek origin, voc. sg. fem. [1]**x**: This appears to be a form of punctuation setting off the vocative **Thyas** from the imperative. [3]**Fortūnātu**: masc. acc. sg. §2.1 Word-final Consonants: **m**.

131. 4637; VI, 15, 6; Vicolo dei Vettii.

1 **Cornelia Hele[na]**

amatur ab · Rufo

132. 4933; VIII, v, 9; Via dell'Abbondanza.

[Ba]lbus et Fortunata duo coiuges

coiugēs: note the use of the prefix **co-** rather than **con-**, cf. **coniugēs**.

133. 5092; IX, v, 11; Via di Nola.

amoris ignes si sentires mulio
magi properares ut videres venerem
diligo iuvenem {puerum} venustum rogo punge iamus
bibisti iamus prende lora et excute
Pompeios defer ubi dulcis est amor
meus es

This graffito is composed in iambic senarii. There is a metrical irregularity in line 2. The fifth foot is a trochee. In line 3 the 1st sg. ending **-o** of the verbs **dīligo** and **rogo** must scan as short, a common feature in imperial poetry. In this same line there is vocalic hiatus between **punge** and **iamus**. In line 5 the verb **est** has aphaeresis of **e**. The text can be divided into 5 syntactic units: (1) lines 1–2; (2) line 3, **dīligo** to **venustum**; (3) lines 3–4, which form a series of requests and commands; (4) lines 5–6, **Pompeiōs** to **meus**; (5) line 6, **es**. The last sentence is unfinished. [1]**sī**: present contrary-to-fact condition. [1]**sentīrēs**: note that the direct object is positioned at the beginning of the line. [1]**mūliō**: voc. sg. masc. [2]**magi**: loss of word-final **s**. Word-final Consonants: **s**. [3]**iuvenem**: written above the line as a correction for **puerum**, which has a line drawn through it. [3]**punge**: supply **mūlōs** as direct object. [3–4]**iāmus**: subjunctive of **eō**, §2.1 Hiatus. [5]**dēfer**: supply the pronoun **mē** as direct object.

134. 5127; IX, iii, 19; Via degli Augustali (east side of Via Stabiana).

Spe{e}s moribus bellis a · VIII ·

Spe{e}s: misspelling for **Spēs**. This is the pet name of a prostitute. **a**: abbrev. for **assibus**.

135. 5251; IX, viii, 11; Vico del Centenario.

Restitutus multas decepit
sepe puellas

[2]**sēpe**: §2.1 Monophthongization, cf. **saepe**.

136. 5358; IX, ?, ?; ?.

Secundus
cum Primigenia
conveniunt

[1]**conveniunt**: the verb is plural by agreement of sense.

137. 6842; VI, xvi, 15; Vicolo dei Vettii.

si quis non vidi Venerem quam pin[xit Apelles]
pupa mea aspiciat talis et i[lla nitet]

The graffito is in the form of an elegiac couplet. [1]**vīdi**: loss of final **t**. §2.1 Word-final Consonants: **t**. Despite the loss of **t**, the final syllable of this word scans as heavy. [1]**[Apellēs]**: name of a painter from Colophon who was famous for his painting of Aphrodite rising from the sea. He was a contemporary of Alexander the Great. [2]**pūpa mea**: §2.1 Word-final Consonants: **m**. In order for the pentameter to scan properly, the two vowels of the pronominal adjective **mea** must be scanned as single syllable (synizesis) and this vowel then elides before the following vowel.

138. 7086; V, ?, 6–7; Via delle Nozze d'Argento (?).

Marcus Spedusa amat

Spedūsa: acc. sg. fem., §2.1 Nasal + Stop Consonant and §2.1 Word-final Consonants: **m**, cf. **Spendūsam**.

139. 8259; I, x, 3; Via del Tempio d'Iside.

Successus textor amat coponiaes ancilla

nomine Hiredem quae quidem illum
non curat sed ille rogat | illa comiseretur
scribit rivalis vale

This graffito has three syntactic units: (1) lines 1–3, **Successus** to **cūrat**; (2) line 3, **sed** to **comiserētur**; (3) line 4. Two lines were added at the end by a different writer, but they are difficult to interpret and so are not included here. [1]**cōpōniaes**: gen. sg. fem., §2.2 1st Declension Genitive Singular. [1]**ancilla**: §2.1 Word-final Consonants: **m**, cf. **ancillam**. [2]**Hīredem**: cognomen of Greek origin. **H** is added by hypercorrection, §2.1 **h**. Note also medial **e** for **i**, cf. **Īridem**. [3]**comiserētur**: subjunctive in indirect command after **rogat**. Double **m** is spelled with a single **m**, cf. **commiserētur**.

140. 8356; I, x, 4; Vicolo del Menandro.

Nucerea quaeres ad porta Romana
in vico Venerio Novelliam
Primigeniam

[1]**Nūcereā**: note **e** for original **i** in hiatus, cf. **Nūceriā**. See §2.1 Hiatus and §2.1 Ablative for Locative. [1]**quaeres**: §2.1 Short **i** in Final Syllables. [1]**porta Romana**: §2.1 Word-final Consonants: **m**. [2]**Veneriō**: the district where brothels are located.

141. 8364; I, x, 7; Via del Tempio d' Iside.

Secundus
Prime suae ubi
que isse salute
rogo domna
ut me ames

This graffito has two syntactic units: (1) lines 1–3; (2) lines 4–5. [2]**Prīmē**: dat. sg. fem., §2.1 Monophthongization. [3]**isse**: probably nom. sg. masc., cf. **ipse**, but could also be dat. sg. fem., cf. **ipsae**, rather than **ipsī**. Note the assimilation of **ps** to **ss**. If **isse** is dat. sg. fem., then it also has monophthongization of the diphthong **ae** to **ē** (see **Prīmē**, line 2). [3]**salūte**: acc. sg. fem., §2.1 Word-final Consonants: **m**. Supply the verb **dīcit**. [4]**domna**: voc. sg. fem., cf. **domina**. §2.1 Syncope.

142. 9123; IX, xiii, 4; Via dell' Abbondanza.

nihil durare potest tempore perpetuo
cum bene sol nituit redditur Oceano
decrescit Phoebe quae modo plena fuit
ven[to]rum feritas saepe fit aura levis

This graffito is written in dactylic pentameters. [1]**nihil**: this word scans as a single heavy syllable. [1]**dūrāre**: 'to remain unchanged.' [1]**tempore perpetuō**: ablative of duration of time. [2]**redditur**: reflexive in meaning + dat., 'return itself to.' [3]**Phoebē**: nom. sg. fem. with Greek inflection, 'the moon.' [3]**modo**: adv., 'a little while ago.'

143. 10234; necropolis, Porta di Nocera; Via di Nocera.

amo te facilis
fac mi copia

[2]**mī**: dat. sg. of **ego**. [2]**cōpia**: acc. sg. fem., §2.1 Word-final Consonants: **m**.

144. 10241; necropolis, Porta di Nocera; Via di Nocera.

Primigeniae
Nucer · sal
vellem essem gemma ora non amplius una
ut tibi signanti oscula pressa darem

This graffito has two parts: (1) a salutation, lines 1–2; (2) an elegiac couplet, lines 3–4. [1–2]Supply the verb **dīcō**. [2]**Nūcer**: abbrev. for **Nūcerīnae**, 'from Nuceria,' dat. sg. fem. [3]Compare II, 7, 146. [3]**vellem**: potential subjunctive, imperfect tense, 'I should have wished.' Word-final **-em** remains in hiatus for metrical reasons. [3]**essem**: this word is governed by **vellem** even though there is no subordinating conjunction. [3]**gemma**: 'seal-stone' of a ring. [3]**ōrā**: Loss of **h**. §2.1 **h**. [3]**ōrā . . . ūnā**: ablative of duration of time. [4]**signantī**: hiatus remains between **signantī** and **oscula**. [4]**pressa**: *CIL* IV prints **missa**, but this has been corrected by Solin ·(1973).

145. Giordano 38; ins. occ. 16–19; Via Consulare.

venimus h[oc c]upidi multo magis ire cupimus

set retinet nostros illa puella pedes

This graffito is in the form of an elegiac couplet. Compare graffito II, 1, 1 for form and sentiment. [1]**vēnimus**: perf. act. [1]**cupīmus**: 4th conjugation. [2]**set**: **t** for **d** by hypercorrection, cf. **sed**. See §2.1. Word-final Consonants: **t** and note **quit** for **quid** in II, 7, 119.

146. Giordano 42; ins. occ. 16–19; Via Consulare.

vell essem gemma ora non amplius una
ut tivi signanti oscula pressa dare

This grafitto is the same as the elegaic couplet in II, 7, 144, lines 3–4 above, but note the spelling differences, most particularly **tivi** for **tibi**. [1]**vell**: abbrev. for **vellem**. [2]**tivi**: dat. sg. of **tū** with medial **b** changed to **v**. §2.1 **b** and **v**. **dare**: §2.1 Word-final Consonants: **m**. [2]**pressa**: corrected from **missa** by Solin (1975).

147. Giordano 45; ins. occ. 16–19; Via Consulare.

felicem somnum qui tecum nocte quiescet
hoc ego si facere multo felicior esse

This graffito is composed in dactylic hexameters. [1]Line 1 is best interpreted as a question introduced by interrogative **quī**, nom. sg. masc. [1]**fēlīcem somnum**: internal accusative after **quiēscet**. Translate 'sleeps a blessed sleep.' [1]**quiēscet**: probably present tense. §2.1 Short **i**. [2]Present contrary-to-fact condition. [2]**hoc**: refers to the event described in line 1. This word scans as metrically heavy. [2]**facere, esse**: 1st sg. impf. subj. with loss of final **m**. §2.1 Word-final Consonants: **m**.

8. Citations from Latin Poets

148. 1893; VIII, i, 2; Basilica, Via Marina.

surda · sit · oranti · tua · ianua · laxa · ferenti
audiat · exclusi · verba · receptus · [a]man[s]

Ovid, *Amores* I.8.77–78. Elegiac couplet.

149. 1894; VIII, i, 2; Basilica, Via Marina.

ianitor · ad · dantis · vigilet · si · pulsat · inanis
surdus · in · obductam · somniet · usqu[e] seram

Propertius, V.5.47–48. Elegiac couplet. [1]**dantīs**: acc. pl. masc. The manuscripts of this poem have **dantēs**. [1]**pulsat**: the manuscripts have subjunctive **pulset**. [2]**somniet**: the subject is **ianitor**.

150. 1895; VIII, i, 2; Basilica, Via Marina.

quid pote tan · durum saxso aut · quid mollius unda
dura tamen molli saxsa cavantur aqua

Ovid, *Ars Amatoria* I.475–476. Elegiac couplet. [1]The manuscripts give the first half of line 1 (475) as **quid magis est saxō dūrum**. [1]**pote**: indecl. adj., 'able,' supply **est**. [1]**tan**: assimilation of word-final **m** to **n** before **d** of **dūrum**. [1]**saxsō**: abl. of comparison rather than **quam saxum**. The two phrases, **tam dūrum quam saxum** and **magis dūrum saxō**, have been conflated. Occasionally the digraph **xs** spells the consonant cluster **ks**. The reason seems to be the idea that two consonants should be spelled by two letters. [2]**mollī**: abl. sg. fem. modifying **aquā**.

151. 1950; VIII, i, 2; Basilica, Via Marina.

quisquis amator erit Scythiae licet ambulet oris
nemo adeo ut feriat barbarus esse volet

Propertius, IV.16.13–14. Elegiac couplet. [1]**Scythiae**: in the manuscripts the form is **Scythicīs**. [2]**feriat**: the manuscripts have the verb **noceat**.

152. 1982, add. pg. 214; VII, ix, Eumachia; Vico dei Scheletri.

carminibus
Circe socios
mutavit
Olyxis

Vergil, *Eclogues* VIII.70. Dactylic hexameter. [4]**Olyxis**: gen. sg. masc., 'Odysseus.' **Olyxis** is most likely a contamination of Οὐλίξης and

ʾΟδυσσεύς. In the manuscripts the name is spelled **Ulixī**, gen. sg. masc. of **Ulixēs, -ī**.

153. 2310k, add. pg. 216; VII, ii, 21 (?); Vicolo di Panattiere.

tu · dea tu prese nostro succurre labore

Vergil, *Aeneid* IX.404. Dactylic hexameter. This is the first line of the prayer of Nisus to the goddess Diana. **prēsē**: the manuscripts have **praesēns**. Note the monophthongization of **ae**, cf. §2.1 Monophthongization. **labōrē**: final **ē** here is probably a mistake for a dative singular spelled by **ei** = **ī**. It is also possible, though less likely, that **labōrē** has the old dative singular spelling **ē**, which is preserved for example in the phrase **iūrē dicendō**. The manuscripts have **labōrī**.

154. 3072; VIII, i, 2; Basilica; Via Marina.

Aeneadum genetrix

Lucretius, *De Rerum Natura* I.1. Beginning of a dactylic hexameter. The remainder of the line reads **hominum dīvomque voluptās**.

155. 3135; VII, ii, 17 (?); Vicolo del Panattiere.

Romulus in caelo

Ennius, *Liber I Annalium* 110 (115). Beginning of dactylic hexameter. The rest of the sentence reads **cum dīs genitālibus aevom | dēgit**.

156. 3149; IX, ii, 24–25 (?); Vico di Balbo.

militat omnes

Ovid, *Amores* I.9.1. **omnes**: nom. sg. masc., §2.1 Short **i**. Beginning of dactylic hexameter. The rest of the line reads **amāns et habet sua castra Cupīdō**.

157. 4491; VI, xiii, 19; Vicolo dei Vettii.

1 **nunc · est · ira · recens · nunc · est · disc[edere tempus]**
2 **si dolor afuerit · crede redibit [amor]**

Propertius, II.5.9–10. Elegiac couplet.

158. 4832; VII, xv, 8, Vicolo del Gallo.

[ar]ma virumque cano Troia<e> qui primus ab oris

Vergil, *Aeneid* I.1. Dactylic hexameter. **Trōia<e>**: the graffito reads **Trōia**.

159. 9131; IX, xiii, 5; Via dell'Abbondanza.

fullones ululamque cano non arma virumq

[Facsimile 19] Parody of line 1 of Vergil's *Aeneid*. The line scans as a dactylic hexameter. **virumq**: abbrev. for **virumque**. For the association of launderers and the screech owl, see II, 1, 17. See also Varro, *Men.* 539: **hominēs eum peius formī dant quam fullō**.

160. Giordano & Casale 71; I, xv, 3; Via di Castricio.

1 **Severus**
2 **mille meae Siculis errant in montibus ag**

[1]**Severus**: supply **scrībit**. [2]Vergil, *Eclogues* II.21. Dactylic hexameter. [2]**ag**: abbreviation for **agnae**.

9. Miscellaneous Graffiti

161. 1291, add. pg. 463; VI, x, 1-3; Via di Mercurio.

da fridam pusillum

Incised above a drawing of a soldier holding out a cup to his servant. **frīdam**: from **frīgidam**, 'cold water,' probably via a change of **g** to **y** before **i**, which was then followed by syncope of medial **i**. **pusillum**: acc. sg. neut., 'a little bit,' in apposition to **frīdam**.

162. 1292, add. pg. 463; VI, x, 1–3; Via di Mercurio.

adde · calicem · Setinum [h]av[e]

Incised next to a figure of a boy holding out a cup. **calicem**: 'cupful of wine.' **Sētīnum**: 'from Setia,' acc. sg. masc. **[h]av[e]**: §2.1 **h**. The verb is inscribed at some distance from **Sētīnum**.

163. 1321, add. pg. 206; VI, ix, ?; Via di Mercurio.

P · Comicius Restitutus cum fratre
ic · stetit

[2]**īc**: §2.1 **h**.

164. 1435; VI, xi, 10; Vico di Mercurio.

[feli]x [es]t · Ianuarius
Fuficius qui hic habitat

165. 1544, add. pg. 263; VI, xiv, 38; Vico dei Vettii.

M Vinicius Vitalis exit pr Non Iulias Afreno et Africano cos

The graffito is dated to AD 59.

166. 1555; VI, xiii, 2; Via della Fortuna.

L Nonio Asprenate
A · Plotio cos Assellus natus
pridie Nonas · Capratinas

The graffito is dated to AD 29. [2]**Assellus**: used here as a term of endearment. Double spelling of medial **s** perhaps by way of hypercorrection since there is some evidence for reduction of **ss**, even after short vowels, cf. **asellus**. [3]**Nōnās Capratīnās**: refers to July 6, the day on which Rome was saved by slave-women from an invasion by neighboring tribes. **Capratīnās**: the usual form is **Caprōtīnās**. Medial **a** (or **ā** ?) for **ō** is probably due to the influence of **capra**, 'nanny-goat.'

167. 1589; V, i, 4–5 (?); Via di Nola.

Aprodite issa

Aprodītē: nom. sg. fem. with Greek inflection. Note that the original Greek aspirated **ph** is spelled as **p** in Latin. **issa**: nom. sg. fem. with assimilation of **ps** to **ss**, cf. **ipsa**. Here the pronominal form indicates eminence, e.g., 'the great one.' For the use of the pronoun, compare II, 5, 83.

168. 1604; V, ii, 3 (?); Via di Nola.

queres
Fallacem · et
Fabium in decuria
Cotini

[1]**quēres**: §2.1 Monophthongization and §2.1 Short **i**, cf. **quaeris**. Interpretation of this form as a future (**quērēs**) is also possible here.

169. 1650; VII, v, 24; Via del Foro.

C · Iulius · [Pri]migenius · hic
tu quid · moraris

[1]Supply the verb **fuit**.

170. 1783; VIII, i, 2; Basilica, Via Marina.

Philodamus · fuit Craudeli Fes
nunc est · Mari · M ser

[1]**Craudēlī**: possibly an error for **Crūdēlī**. [1]**Fes**: abbrev. for **Festī**. Supply **servus** as noun governing the genitives. [2]**M**: note the position of the praenomen following the nomen. [2]**ser**: abbrev. for **servus**.

171. 1831; VIII, i, 2; Basilica, Via Marina]

si quisquis · bibit cetera turba · est

172. 1842; VIII, i, 2; Basilica; Via Marina.

C · Pumidius · Dipilus · heic · fuit
a · d V · Nonas Octobreis · M · Lepid · Q · Catul cos
cum

The graffito is dated to October 3, 88 BC. [1]**heic**: §2.1 Long Vowels. [2]**Octobreis**: acc. pl. fem., §2.1 Long Vowels. [3]**cum**: the graffito is unfinished.

173. 1847; VIII, i, 2; Basilica, Via Marina.

Rufio – Sitti – P ser a d X K A
haec nav[e] pinxset C Caesare P Serv
[c]os

The graffito is dated to July 23, 48 BC. It is next to a drawing of a ship. [1]**Rufio**: nom. sg. masc., §2.1 Word-final Consonants: **s**. [1]**ser**: abbrev. for **servus**, which governs the genitive, **Sittī P** (= **Pūblī Sittī**). [1]**a d X K A**: abbreviations for **ante diem X Kalendās Augustās**. [2]**haec**: the nominative is a mistake for accusative. [2]**nave**: §2.1 Word-final Consonants: **m**. [2]**pinxset**: §2.1 Short **i**. Note the spelling **xs** for **x** = [ks]; cf. **saxsa** II, 8, 150 with note. [3]**[c]os**: abbrev. for **cōnsulibus**.

174. 1870, add. pg. 464; VIII, i, 2; Basilica, Via Marina.

minimum · malum · fit contemnendo · maxumum · menedemerumenus

See III, 2, 11 and compare the maxim of Publius Syrus: **necesse est minima maximōrum esse initiō**. The maxim is in the form of an iambic senarius. **maxumum**: §2.1 Medial **i** and **u**. **menedemerumenus**: it is not clear what this Greek-sounding word refers to, if anything.

175. 1880; VIII, i, 2; Basilica, Via Marina.

L · Istacidi · at · quem · non ceno · barbarus · ille · mihi · est

[Facsimile 20] **L · Istacidī**: voc. sg. masc. **at**: assimilation of word-final **d** (voiced) to word-initial **qu** (voiceless), §2.1 Word-final Consonants: **t**. Here **at** has the meaning of **apud**, 'at the house of.' **quem**: the antecedent is **ille**. **mihi**: dative of reference.

176. 1896; VIII, i, 2; Basilica, Via Marina.

ubi · perna cocta · est · si convivae apponitur
non gustat pernam ' lingit · ollam · aut · caccabum

This graffito is composed in iambic senarii. [2]The function of the vertical dash separating **pernam** and **lingit** is unclear although it does mark the division between the two verb phrases in this line.

177. 1899, add. pg. 213; VIII, i, 2; Basilica, Via Marina.

hominem reddit rhetor – qui emit
servom [doctu]m os non habet

The graffito is written in trochaic septenarius. [1]–: the punctuation here separates two sentences. [2]**servom**: **o** is occasionally written for **u** after **v**.

178. 1904, add. pg. 213; VIII, i, 2; Basilica, Via Marina.

admiror o pariens te · non cecidisse [ruini]s · qui tot
scriptorum ta[ed]ia sustineas

This graffito is in the form of an elegiac couplet. The hexameter ends with **[ruīnī]s**. [1]**o**: particle of exclamation with the vocative **pariēns**. If **o** is the correct reading, the particle is extra-metrical. In the *Addenda et Corrigenda* to Vol. 1, pg. 213, the editor suggests that **o** may actually be a word-punct, in which case the hexameter has no metrical irregularities. [1]**pariēns**: voc. sg. fem. The **n** is written before **ē** by hypercorrection. §2.1 **ns**. [2]**sustineās**: subjunctive mood in a relative clause of characteristic. Compare II, 9, 185, which is cited below.

179. 2016; VII, xi, 11; Vico del Balcone Pensile.

mulus hic · muscellas docuit

[Facsimile 21] This graffito describes teacher and students. **muscellās**: the *OLD* defines this word as 'little mules,' but **muscella** cannot be a diminutive formation from **mulus**. A better interpretation is that **muscella** is derived from **musca**, 'fly,' and that it refers here to small and troublesome flies or gnats.

180. 2069; VIII, iv, 4; Via dell' Abbondanza.

moram si quaeres
sparge miliu et col
lige

[1]**quaeres**: §2.1 Short **i**, cf. **quaeris**. **miliu**: §2.1 Word-final Consonants: **m**.

181. 2119; VIII, iv, 12 (?); Via dell' Abbondanza.

vici Nuceriae
in alia · * DCCCLVs
fide bona

[1]**Nūceriae**: loc. sg. fem. [2]**aliā**: abl. sg. fem., cf. **aleā**. §2.1 Hiatus. [2]*****: symbol for **dēnāriōs**.

182. 2258a; VII, xii, 18; Vico del Lupanare.

Africanus moritur
scribet · puer Rusticus
condisces cui dolet pro Africano

[2]**scrībet**: §2.1 Short **i**, cf. **scrībit**. [2]**puer**: with the meaning 'slave.' [3]**condiscēs**: pres. act. part., 'school chum,' §2.1 **ns**. [3]**cuī**: possibly nom. sg. masc. with **c** for **q**. If **cuī** is dat. sg. masc., then **dolet** is to be treated as an impersonal.

183. 2331; IX, iii, 5; Via Stabiana.

labyrinthus
hic · habitat
Minotaurus

See Facsimile on title page. [1]**labyrinthus**: this word is a label for the drawing.

184. 2351; IX, ii, 4; Via Stabiana.

Polucarpus fugit

Polucarpus: the name of a slave or perhaps a gladiator.

185. 2487; II, 7; Amphitheatre.

ad · miror te · paries · non c[e]cidisse
qui tot · scriptorum taedia sustineas

See II, 9, 178. [1]**ad · miror**: the interpunct separating the preverb from the verb could be an error but there are other examples of this type of punctuation.

186. 3123; VII, ii, 16 or iii, 25 (?); Vicolo del Panettiere.

Antiochus Liviaes · ser
[A]ntio[c]hus · Liviae · s[e]r

[1]**Liviaes**: gen. sg. fem., §2.2 1st Declension Genitive Singular. [1–2]**ser**: abbrev. for **servus**. Was line 2 of this grafitto, in which the genitive has the classical Latin form, offered as a correction to line 1?

187. 3129; VII, ii, 16 or iii, 25 (?); Vicolo del Panettiere.

cadaver mortus

cadāver: note that the gender is masculine, not neuter. **mortus**: loss of **u** before the vowel **u**, cf. **mortuus**.

188. 3146; VII, ii, 16 or iii, 25 (?); Vicolo di Panettiere.

1 **Secundus**
2 **[[hi<c> cacat]]**
3 **[[h[i<c> ca]cat]]**
4 **[[hic cacat]]**

[2–3]**hī<c> cacat**: the graffito, which is written *scriptio continua*, reads **hīcacat**, so the initial **c** of **cacat** does double duty standing also for the final **c** of **hīc**. Lines 2–4 seem to have been erased in antiquity.

189. 4107; V, ii, 4; Via di Nola.

1 **fullo**
2 **L · Quintilius ·**
3 **Cresces hic**
4 **regnatus · est**

For **Crescēs** see II, 1, 15–17. [4]**regnātus · est**: translate 'held sway, governed.'

190. 4278; V, v, 2; Via di Nola.

1 **fures ·**
2 **faras   r**
3 **frugi · intro**

[2]**farās**: **a** in the first syllable is either an error or changed from **o** by vocalic assimilation, cf. **forās**. The spelling **farās** is attested also in an inscription from Rome. [2]**r**: this letter seems not to be connected to our graffito. [3]**frūgī**: indecl. adj. used substantively.

191. 4429; VI, v, 10; Vicolo di Modesto.

M · Iuni · insula · sum

192. 4456; VI, xiii, 6; Via della Fortuna.

1 **semper · M · Terentius Eudoxsus**

2 **unus · supstenet amicos · et · tenet**
3 **et · tutat · supstenet · omne · modu**

It is claimed that this graffito scans as an elegiac couplet if **supstenet**, line 2, is omitted from consideration. Other metrical infelicities remain. **Eudoxsus**, line 1, must scan as a dactyl, and **omne**, line 3, must scan as a trochee. [1]**Eudoxsus**: occasionally the digraph **xs** spells the consonant cluster **ks**. [2–3]**supstenet**: with etymological spelling of the preverb, cf. **sustineō**. The medial **e** in this verb, rather than expected **i**, is probably due to the influence of uncompounded **tenet** in line 2, but Pompeiian graffiti also attest to confusion between short **e** and **i** in unaccented medial syllables. [2]**tenet**: 'hold (by ties of allegiance or affection).' [3]**tūtat**: deponent in classical Latin, but active forms are attested in Old Latin writers, e.g., Plautus, Naevius, Pomponius, etc. Note asyndeton between **tūtat** and **supstenet**. [3]**omne modu**: probably acc. sg. masc. with adverbial function, 'in every way,' cf. **omnī modō** abl. sg. masc.

193. 4533; VI, xiv, 37; Vicolo dei Vettii.

1 **G Hadius Ventrio**
2 **eques natus Romanus inter**
3 **beta et brassica**

[Facsimile 22] [2]**eques . . . Rōmānus**: in apposition to the name in line 1. [2]**nātus**: supply **est**. [3]**bēta**: acc. sg. fem., §2.1 Word-final Consonants: **m**. [3]**brassica**: acc. sg. fem., §2.1 Word-final Consonants: **m**.

194. 4600; VI, xv, 1; Vicolo dei Vettii.

oc Celer fecite

oc: §2.1 **h**. **fēcite**: final **e** by addition of prop vowel or by misspelling There is some evidence for loss of final **t** in Pompeiian inscriptions so the addition of a prop vowel to to impede the loss of final **t** has some support. See §2.1 Word-final Consonants: **t**.

195. 4603; VI, xv, 1; Vicolo dei Vettii.

Romanus olim palim aurum pro ferrum dedica

palim: 'again, once more.' This word was borrowed from Greek πάλιν. The final **m** in **palim**, rather than **n**, is due to the influence of **olim**. **prō**: §2.4 Prepositions. **dēdica**: probably loss of word-final **t**. §2.1 Word-Final **t**.

196. 4719; VII, vii, 5; Via Marina.

Restitutus ·
servos · bo
nus

[2]**servos**: nom. sg. masc., cf. **servus**.

197. 4755; VII, vii, 5; Via Marina.

Cresces architectus

Crescēs: §2.1 **ns**.

198. 4777; VII, vii, 5; Via Marina.

Confirminus
L Ot{·t}acilius moritur

[1]**Confirmīnus**: supply the verb **scrībit**. [2]**Ot{·t}acilius**: misspelling for **Otacilius**.

199. 4925; VII, iii, 9; Via della Fortuna.

Anteros hoc · scripsit

Anteros: cognomen of Greek origin, nom. sg. masc. The name has Greek *o*-stem inflection.

200. 4957, add. pg. 705; VIII, vii, 6; Via Stabiana.

miximus in lecto fateor peccavimus
hospes si dices quare nulla matella fuit

This graffito is composed in an elegaic couplet. The pentameter begins with the word **sī** in line 2. [1]**miximus**: compare the perfect **minxī** with nasal from present tense **mingō**. [2]**dīces**: §2.1 Short **i**, cf. **dīcis**.

201. 4999, IX, ii, 26; Via degli Augustali.

> **M · Casellium Marcellum aedilem bonum et munerarium magnum**

Graffito in the form of an electoral announcement. Supply the verb phrase **ōrō vōs faciātis**. For **Casellius Marcellus** see I, 1, 9.

202. 5009; IX, ii, 26; Via degli Augustali (east side of Via Stabiana).

> **felices omnes frustraque vocantur quem sufferre potest nemo**

quem: the antecedent, **omnēs**, is plural.

203. 5011; IX, ii, 26; Via degli Augustali (east side of Via Stabiana).

> **lector an mathematicus an rhetoricos**

lector: voc. sg. masc. **rhetoricos**: nom. sg. masc. with Greek inflection. Supply the verb **es**.

204. 5065; IX, iii, 19; Via degli Augustali.

> **hic domus Papiriu Sabinium**

hīc domus: supply **est** and take **domus**, 'town house,' as predicate noun. **Papiriū Sabīniūm**: gen. sg. masc. with Greek inflection, **-ū** = -ου. The **m** in **Sabīniūm** is added by hypercorrection. See §2.1 Word-final Consonants: **m**.

205. 5112; IX, v, 18; street between IX, v and IX, vi.

> **discite dum vivo mors**
> **inimica venis**

The graffito scans as a dactylic pentameter. It has two parts: (1) line 1 **discite**; (2) lines 1-2, **dum** to **venīs**. [1]**discite**: supply a direct object pronoun **hoc**, which refers to the following sentence. [1]**mors**: voc. sg. fem.

206. 5214; IX, vii, 3–6; Vico del Centenario.

Officiosus fugit VIII · Idus · Nov
Druso Caesare M Iunio Silano cos

[Facsimile 23] The name of the slave **Officiōsus** means 'dutiful.' The graffito is dated to AD 15.

207. 5244; IX, vii, 3-6; Via del Centenario(?).

Marthae hoc trichilinium
est · nam in · trichilinio
cacat

[1]**trīchilīnium**: Greek τρικλίνιον is the source of this Latin word. **ch** stands for **c** despite the fact that this word did not have an aspirate in it. The medial **i** standing between **ch** and **l** is an epenthetic vowel. [2]**trichilīniō**: for spelling and epenthetic vowel see note 1.

209. 6702; V, iii, 9; Vico di Lucretio Frontone.

Aufidius · hic fuit va

210. 6796; V, iv, a; Vico di Lucretio Frontone.

M · Lucretius · Fronto · vir · fortis
[[et ho]]

[2]**[[ho]]**: perhaps the scriptor began to write **honestus**? This line is scratched out.

211. 6838; VI, xvi, 10; Via del Vesuvio.

IX K Iunias inperator
dies fuit Solis

The date is May 24, AD 61 or AD 67. Nero is emperor. **inperator**: etymological spelling for **imperator**. Supply the verb phrase **hīc fuit**.

212. 7065; V, iv, south side; Via di Nola.

> **aedilem · Procul{u}m [[cr]] cunctorum · turba probavit · hoc pudor ingenuus · postulavit · et · pietas**

Graffito supporting the political candidacy of **Publius Paquius Proculus**. See I, 1, 11. The graffito has two sentences. The second sentence begins with **hoc**. **Procul{u}m**: the inscription reads **Proculam**. **[[cr]]**: error for the beginning of **cūnctōrum**. These letters were erased by the scriptor.

213. 8149; I, vii, 7; Via dell'Abbondanza.

> **na[t]us Cornelius Sabinus**

nā[t]us: supply **est**.

214. 8162; I, vii, 8; Via Stabiana.

> **hic · fuimus · cari · duo · nos · sine fine sodales**
> **nomina · si**

The first line of this graffito is composed of a dactylic hexameter. Line 2 is incomplete. One editor suggests completing line 2 as follows: **quaeris Caius et Aulus erant**. The second line then scans as a dactylic pentameter and the whole graffito is in the form of an elegaic couplet.

215. 8417; I, xi, 2; Via dell'Abbondanza.

> **bonus deus**
> **hic abitat in do**
> **mo**
> **Act**

[1]**bonus deus**: the god Hercules. [2]**abitat**: §2.1 **h**. [4]**Āct**: abbrev. for **Āctī**, gen. sg. masc. of **Āctius**.

216. 8562; II, vii; Palaestra.

qui mihi · docendi
dederit mercedem
abeat quod
petit · a superis

[Facsimile 24] [1]**docendī**: gen. sg. neut., 'for teaching.' [3]**abeat**: §2.1 **h**. [4]**superīs**: abl. pl. masc. used as substantive.

217. 8660; II, 7, Palaestra.

Pacatus
hic · cum suis
masit Pompeis

[3]**māsit**: §2.1 **ns**, cf. **mānsit**.

218. 8820; III, ii, 1; Via dell' Abbondanza.

X K Febra
Ursa · peperit diem
Iovis

[1]**X K Febra**: abbrev. for **X Kalendās Febr(u)āriās**. [2]**Ursa**: a pet name. [2]**diēm**: abl. sg. fem. with addition of final **m** by hypercorrection. See §2.1 Word-final Consonants: **m**.

219. 8976; XIV, iv, 4; Via di Nola.

Progamus cum iumentum

cum: §2.4 Prepositions. Supply the verb phrase **hīc fuit**.

220. 9226; Villa dei Misteri.

Rufus est

221. 10093c; II, iv, 10; street between II, iv and II, iii.

Bru[t]us canis est

This is the reading suggested tenatively by Solin (1973). The reading given in *CIL* IV is suspect.

222. 10202; VI, iii, 5; Via Consolare.

VI K Sep masimus
Popeis

[1]**māsimus**: §2.1. **ns**, cf. **mānsimus**. [2]**Popeīs**: loss of **m** before **p**, §2.1 Nasal + Stop Consonant.

III. DIPINTI AND GRAFFITI FROM HERCULANEUM

1. Dipinti

1. 10488; Castellum Aquarium; crossroads of Cardo IV & Decumanus Maximus.

M · [Alf]icius Pa[ul]lus
aedil
[siqu]is · velit · in hunc · locum
stercus · abicere · monetur · n[on]
iacere · siquis · adver[sus hoc]
idicium · fecerit · liberi dent
[dena]rium · n · servi · verberibus
[. . . i]n · sedibus · admonentur

This dipinto is an ordinance sponsored by the aedile **Marcus Alficius Paullus** aimed at prohibiting the dumping of excrement near a water reservoir and the public fountain adjacent to it. The text was painted in black letters on a whitewashed wall of a water reservoir located at the crossroads of the Decumanus Maximus and Cardo III, between the northern corners of blocks VI and VII. The inscription has 3 parts: (1) lines 1–2, name of the sponsor; (2) lines 3–5, **[sīqu]is** to **iacere**, prohibition (3) lines 5–8, **sīquis** to **admonentur**, punishments for violation of the prohibition. [2]**aedīl**: abbrev. for **aedīlis**. [6]**idicium**: loss of **n** before **d**, see §2.1 Nasal + Stop Consonant. [7]**n**: abbrev. for **nummum**, gen. pl. masc. [8]**[. . . i]n**: it seems likely that a number indicating the quantity of lashes (**verberibus**) has been lost. [8]**sēdibus**: it is not clear what this word means in this context. It has been suggested that **sēdibus** here refers to the 'buttocks' and thus that slaves are to be punished by being whipped on the buttocks for violating this prohibition. This seems unlikely, however, since there is no evidence that slaves were so beaten.

2. Pagano; Decumanus Maximus.

M · Caecili
Potitum
quaestor
[– – –]

[1]**Caecili**: abbrev. for **Caecilium**. [3]**quaestōr**: abbreviation for **quaestōrem**. The rest of the inscription is missing. This inscription could be an electoral announcement, in which case one would expect the formulaic phrase **o v f** followed by the name or names of supporters. However, there is no example at Pompeii of an electoral inscription in which one of the candidates stands for the office of quaestor.

2. Graffiti

3. 10502; iii, 14.

Vasileus habitat
Putelis in castris August[i]
su Valeri[o]

This graffito was written by a soldier stationed at Puteoli. [1]**Vasileus**: initial **V** in this name is suspect. Perhaps **Basileus** was written. [2]**Putelīs**: abl. sg. fem., 'at Puteoli.' [3]**su**: loss of final **b**, cf. **sub**, 'under the command of.'

4. 10528; iv, 15–16.

Euhodus
et Satura
Puteolani

Incised beneath the figures of two gladiators in combat. **Puteolānī**: nom. pl. masc., 'from Puteoli.'

5. 10565; v, 7.

vinum acceptum
ab domino VII Idus Apriles

This graffito probably records a ration of wine given to servants.

6. 10566; v, 7.

aquaria · dua cum basis
aqua in manus · dua cum basis

3 hamas · duas · cum basis
4 aqua in manu cotidianu I
5 cum basis
6 urciolos duos
7 candelabra quatuor
8 et lucubratoriu unum
9 lucerna aenea
10 hamula · una
11 pelvi cum basim
12 et lytrum
13 gutos tres
14 scapheola dua
15 ferrea strigles VII
16 haenas quattuor
17 marmor cum basim
18 aenea
19 fulminaria dua

This graffito is an inventory of types of household items, primarily vessels and bowls of various sorts. Note that these items are listed in the accusative case. See §2.4 Accusative in Lists. [1]**dua**: acc. pl. neut. The neuter form is probably modeled on the neuter **tria**, 'three.' [1]**cum**: + acc. pl., §2.4 Prepositions. [1]**basīs**: acc. pl. fem. [2]**aquā**: abbrev. for **aquāria**. [3]**hamās**: a borrowing from Greek. The **h** is unetymological. §2.1 **h**. [4]**aquā**: abbrev. for **aquārium**. [4]**manū**: acc. pl. fem., §2.1 Word-final Consonants: **s**. **dua**: acc. pl. neut. [4]**cotīdiānu**: acc. sg. neut., probably in the sense 'ordinary.' [6]**urciolōs**: short **e** changed to **i** in hiatus, cf. **urceolōs**. §2.1 Hiatus. [7]**quatuor**: note the single spelling of **t**. [8]**lūcubrātōriu**: acc. sg. neut., 'night-light.' [9]**lucerna aenea**: acc. sg. fem. §2.1 Word-final Consonants: **m**. [10]**hamula una**: acc. sg. fem. §2.1 Word-final Consonants: **m**. [11]**pelvi**: acc. sg. fem., §2.1 Word-final Consonants: **m**. [12]**lytrum**: 'wash-basin.' [14]**scapheola**: acc. fem. sg., probably 'small wash-basin or tub,' cf. **scaphium**, 'small concave-shaped basin.' Note that the **e** in hiatus stands for original **i**. See §2.1 Word-final Consonants: **m** and §2.1 Hiatus. [15]**ferreā**: acc. pl. fem. Since this line is written as **ferreāstrigīēs**, it is possible that medial **s** serves double-duty, as the final for **ferreās** and the intial for **striglēs**. [15]**striglēs**: syncope of medial **i**, cf. **strigilēs**. §2.1 Syncope. [16]**haēnās**: 'bronze vessels.' Initial **h** is written by hypercorrection, §2.1 **h**. This noun is normally neuter in gender, cf. **ahēnum** 'caldron.' [17]**marmor**: acc. sg. masc., abbrev. for **marmorem**, 'marble basin.' [18]**aēnea**: acc. sg. fem. modifying **basim**. §2.1 Word-final Consonants: **m**. [19]**dua**: acc. pl. neut.

7. 10575; v, 18.

1 **XI K · pane factum**
2 **III Nonas pane factum**

[1–2]**pane**: acc. sg. masc., §2.1 Word-final Consonants: **m**. For the accusatives see §2.4 Accusative in Lists.

8. 10579; v, 30.

1 **VIII K · Martias**
2 **Numisii Genialis**
3 **gladiatorum paria X**
4 **Herculani**

Graffito in the form of a gladiatorial announcement. [2]**Numisiī**: gen. sg. masc. of 2nd Declension noun in **-ius**. The form of the genitive is unusual. See §2.2 2nd Declension Genitive Singular. [4]**Herculānī** loc. sg. neut. of **Herculāneum**. See §2.1 Short **e** and **i** and §2.1 Contraction. Supply the verb **pugnābunt**.

9. 10606; vi, 11.

1 **exemta**
2 **stecora**
3 **a XI**

A memorandum about the cost of the removal of dung. [1]**exēmta**: supply the verb **est**, = **exēmpta est**. [2]**stecora**: cf. **stercora**. For simplification of **rc** cluster see II, 6, 93. [3]**a**: abbreviation for **assibus**, ablative of price.

10. 10631; Insula Orientalis i, 2–3.

1 **Fuibus**
2 **egrotes**

An imprecation. [1]**Fuibus**: spelling of a name **Phoebus**, a cognomen of Greek origin. [2]**ēgrōtes**: 2nd sg. subj., §2.1 Monophthongization, cf. **aegrōtēs**.

11. 10634; Insula Orientalis i, 2–3.

qui · se tutari · nescit · nescit · vivere
minimum · malu · fit contemnendo · maximum

This graffito is written in iambic senarii. [1]**tūtārī**: deponent. [2]**malu**: nom. sg. neut., §2.1 Word-final Consonants: **m**. [2]Compare II, 9, 174.

12. 10664; Insula Orientalis ii, 10.

Septembr
III Idus pro tunica * I a VII

Grafitto recording the purchase of a tunic. [1]**Septembr**: abbrev. for acc. pl. fem. [2]*: the symbol represents the word **dēnārium**. **a**: abbrev. for **assēs**.

13. 10676; Insula Orientalis ii.

Hermeros Primigeniae dominae
veni Puteolos in vico Timniano et quaere
P Messio Numulario Hermerotem Phoebi

A note. [1]**Hermeros**: nom. sg. masc. with Greek inflection; the cognomen is Greek in origin. [1]**Prīmigeniae dominae**: dat. sg. fem. [2]**Timniānō**: name of a neighborhood in Puteoli. [3]**Numulāriō**: the editor of the inscription in *CIL* takes this word as a noun, 'banker.' [3]**Phoebī**: understand **servum**.

14. 10680; Insula Orientalis ii.

mortus
Sumpo

Obituary notice. [1]**mortus**: loss of **u** before a back vowel. [2]**Sumpo**: abbrev. for **Sumpor** or **Sumporus**, a slave name; cf. **Symphorus**.

15. 10697; Vicus sub Insula IV situs.

Fortunatus · amat · Amplianda
Ianuarius · amat · Veneria

rogamus · d<o>mna · Venus
ut · nos · in · mente · habias
quod · te · modo · int<e>ro{r}gamus

[1]**Amplianda**: §2.1 Word-final Consonants: **m**. [2]**Veneria**: §2.1 Word-final Consonants: **m**. [3]**d<o>mna**: voc. sg. fem., cf. **domina**. The inscription reads **damna**. §2.1 Syncope. [3]**Venus:** voc. sg. fem. in apposition with **d<o>mna**. [4]**habias**: §2.1 Hiatus. [5]**modo**: with temporal meaning, 'now.' [5]**int<e>ro{r}gāmus**: the inscription reads **introrgāmus**.

FACSIMILES OF INSCRIPTIONS

Facsimile #1: see pages xii, xxxvi

Facsimile #2: see page xii

M HOLCONIVM

PRISCVM·II VIR·I·D· POMARI·VNIVERSI
CVM·HELVIO·VESTALE·ROG

Facsimile #3: see page xii

D·LVCRETI· (SCR CELER)

SCR AEMILIVS

SATRI·VALENTIS ·FLAMINIS · NERÓNIS· CAESARIS · AVG· FÍLI· CELER · SING

PERPETVÍ·GLADIATÓRVM·PARIA·XX·ET·D·LVCRETIO·VALENTIS·FÍLI· AD LVNA

GLAD·PARIÁ·X·PVG· POMPEÍS·VI·V·IV·III·PR·ÍDVS·APR·VÉNATIÓ·LEGITIMA·

ET·VELA· ERVNT

Facsimile #4: see pages xii, xv

Facsimile #5: see page xix

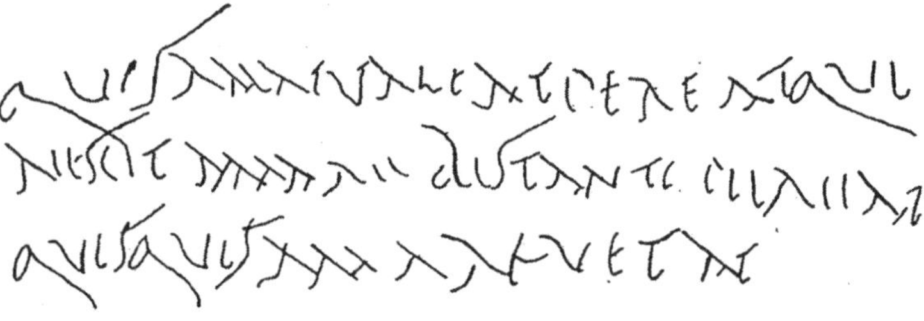

Facsimile #6: see pages xix–xx

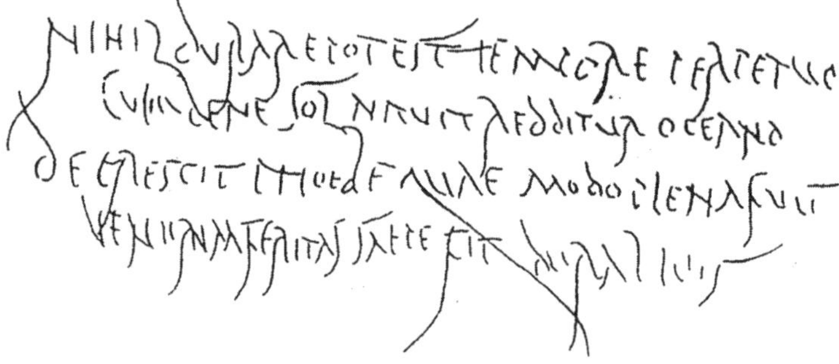

Facsimile #7: see page xxi

Facsimile #8: see page xxii

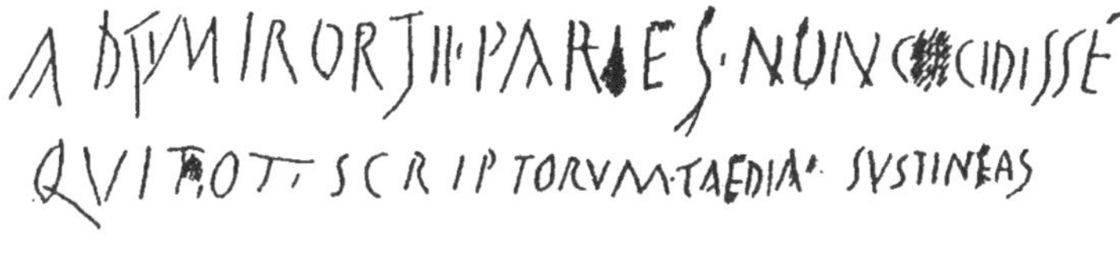

Facsimile #9: see page xxiii

Facsimile #10: see pages xxxvi, 2

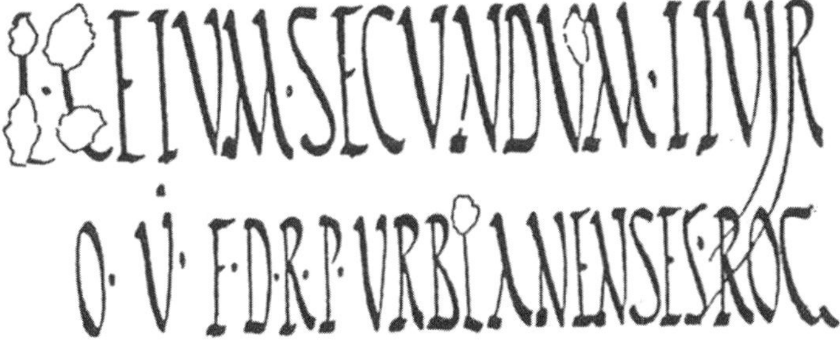

Facsimile #11: see page xxxvi

Facsimile #12: see pages 24–25

Facsimile #13: see page 51

Facsimile #14: see page 57

Facsimile #15: see page 59

Facsimile #16: see page 61

Facsimile #17: see page 61

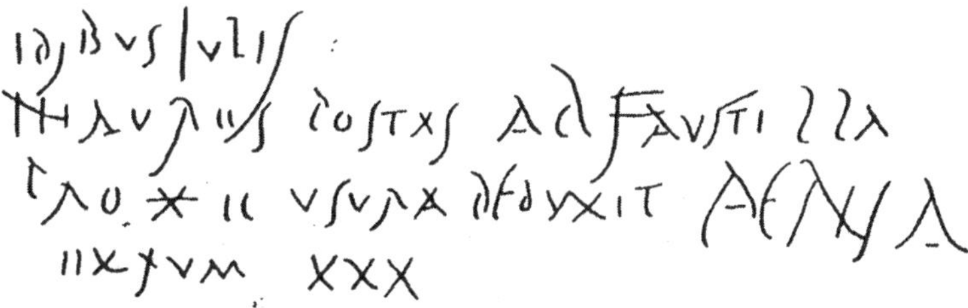

Facsimile #18: see page 70

Facsimile #19: see page 83

Facsimile #20: see page 87

Facsimile #21: see page 88

Facsimile #22: see page 91

Facsimile #23: see page 94

Facsimile #24: see page 96

ABBREVIATIONS IN INSCRIPTIONS

I. Words and Phrases

a v a s p p	aedīlem viīs aedibus sacrīs pūblicīs prōcūrandīs
aed v a s p p	aedīlem viīs aedibus sacrīs pūblicīs prōcūrandīs
aed v a sacr p p	aedīlem viīs aedibus sacrīs pūblicīs prōcūrandīs
a	assēs, assibus
ass	assēs, assibus
a d	ante diem
aed	aedīlem, aedīlēs
Aug	Augustae
Aug	Augustī
Aug	Augustālibus
Aug	Augustās, Augustīs
c	centūriae
c	corōnārum
ch, coh	cohortis
cos	consulibus
*	dēnārius
d, dig, dign	dignus, dignī
d i d, d i dic	duumvirum iūrē dīcendō
d r p	dignum reī pūblicae
d v	duumvirum
II vir	duumvirum
d v i d	duumvirum iūrē dīcundō
II v i d	duumvirum iūrē dīcundō
II vir i d	duumvirum iūrē dīcundō
II vir iur dic	duumvirum iūrē dīcundō
II vir v b d r p	duumvirum virum bonum dignum rei publicae
d v v a s p p	duumvirum viīs aedibus sacrīs pūblicīs prōcūrandīs
II vir v a s p p	duumvirum viīs aedibus sacrīs pūblicīs prōcūrandīs
f	fīlī
f	fīliae
faci	faciātis
fam glad	familia gladiātōria
fam gladiat	familia gladiātōria
fel, felic	fēlīciter

HS	sestertiī, sestertia
glad	gladiātōrum
gl par	gladiātōrum paria
glad par	gladiātōrum paria
i d	iūrē dīcundō
imp	imperātōris
itaq	itaque
Iul	Iūliānus
l	lībertus, lībertum
lib	lībertus, lībertum
libr	lībertus, lībertum
liber	lībertus, lībertum
m ch	mīles cohortis
mil coh	mīles cohortis
m	missus est
N	Nerōniānus
Ner	Nerōniānus
o v f	ōrō vōs faciātis
o v fac	ōrō vōs faciātis
p	perit
p	pondō
p p	patris patriae
par	paria gladiātōrum
pr	prīdiē
pr	praetōriae
pug	pugnābit, pugnābunt
pugn	pugnābit, pugnābunt
pugna	pugnābit, pugnābunt
pugnab	pugnābit, pugnābunt
q	quinquennālis, quinquennālī, quinquennālem
quinq	quinquennālis, quinquennālī, quinquennālem
r	rogat, rogant
r p	reī pūblicae
rei p	reī pūblicae

rog	rogat, rogant
sal	salūtem
salut	salūtem
scr	scrībit
ser	servus, servum
supp	suppositicī
T	Thrāx, Thraex
Tr	Thrāx, Thraex
u	ubique
ubiq	ubique
v	valē
v	vīcit
va	valē
val	valē
v a s p p	viīs aedibus sacrīs pūblicīs prōcūrandīs
v b	virum bonum
vic	vīcit
virum b	virum bonum
ven	vēnālia
ven	vēnātiō
venat	vēnātiō

II. Roman Calendar

Ap, Apr, April	Aprilīs, Aprilibus
Dec	Decembrēs
Eid	Īdūs
Feb, Febr	Februāriās, Februārīs
Id, Idu	Īdūs
Iul	Iūliās
K, Kal	Kalendās, Kalendīs
Mai	Māiās, Māīs
Mart	Mārtiās
Non	Nōnās
Nov, Novembr	Novembrēs

III. Praenomina

A	Aulus, Aulī
C	Gāius, Gāī

Cn	Gnaeus
D	Decius
G	Gāius
Ga	Gāvius
L	Lūcius
M	Mārcus
M′	Manlius
N	Numerius
Q	Quīntus
P	Pūblius
S	Salvius
Sex	Sextus
Sp	Spurius
St	Statius (?)
Ti	Tiberius
T	Titus

IV. Cognomina

Neron	Nerō, Nerōnis
Poly	Polybius, Polybī

V. Cities

Cōnstant · Nūcer	Cōnstantiae Nūceriae
Pom	Pompeīs
Puteōl	Puteōlīs

INDEX OF NAMES

Candidates for the Aedileship

Candidates for the Duumvirate

Other Candidates

Supporters of Candidates

Painters, Whitewashers

Sponsors of Gladiatorial Games

Other Names in Gladiatorial Announcements and Dipinti

Names in Other Dipinti

Names in Graffiti

Names of Divinities and Heroes

Names from Herculaneum

VOCABULARY

A

ā, ab, prep. + abl., *by*
aberrō, -āre, -āvī, -ātum, *to lose; get lost*
abiciō, -ere, -iēcī, -iectum, *to throw away*
abitō, see **habitō**
abominō, -āre, -āvī, -ātum, *to loathe, abhor, despise*
absum, abesse, āfuī, *to be absent*
acervus, -ī, m., *pile, heap, stack*
accipiō, -ere, -cēpī, -ceptum, *to receive*
acua, see **aqua**
acūtus, -a, -um, *sharpened, sharp*
ad, prep. + acc., *near, beside; against*
adeō, adv., so, *to such a degree*
admiror, -ārī, -ātus, *to be surprised*
admoneō, -ēre, -uī, -itum, *to admonish*
adstō, -āre, -stitī, *to stand near, beside*
adulescēns, -entis, m., *young man*
adversus, prep. + acc., *contrary to*
aedēs, -is, f., *building*
aedīlis, aedīlis, m. *aedile*
aegrōtō, -āre, -āvī, -ātum, *to be sick, be ill*
Aeneadēs, -ae, m., (pl.) *descendants of the Trojans* (companions of Aeneas)
aēneus, -a, -um, *of bronze*
aēnius, -a, -um, see **aēneus, -a, -um**
aerārium, ī, n., *treasury*
aes, aeris, n., *cash, money*
aevom, -ī, n., *eternity*
agna, -ae, f., *ewe lamb*
ālia [= ālea], -ae, f., *gambling, game of gambling*
ālium, -ī, n., *garlic plant*
alligō, -āre, -āvī, -ātum, *to bind, tie up, fasten*
amātor, -ōris, m., *lover*
ambulō, -āre, -āvī, -ātum, *to walk*
amīcus, -ī, m., *friend*
amō, -āre, -āvī, -ātum, *to love, to be or fall in love with*
amphithiātrum, -ī, n., *amphitheatre*
amplius, adv., *more*
amphra, -ae, f., *amphora*
ancilla, -ae, f., *maidservant*
ancla, see **ancilla**
anima, -ae, f., *person, friend*
animula, -ae, f., *little life* (as a term of endearment)
annus, -ī, m., *year*
ante, prep. + acc., *before*
appōnō, -ere, -posuī, -positum, *to place beside, place near*
Aprilis, -is, -e, *of April*
Aprodītē, -ēs, f., *Aphrodite*
aqua, -ae, f., *water*
aquārium, -ī, n., *water pitcher*
āra, -ae, f., *altar*
archimīmus, -ī, m., *archimine, chief of troop of mimic actors*
architectus, -ī, m., *architect*
ardaliō [= ardeliō], -ōnis, m., *busy-body*
arma, -ōrum, n. pl., *weapons*
Arriānus Polliānus, -a, -um, *belonging to Arrius Pollio*
as, assis, m., *a penny, a coin of small value*
asellus, -ī, *ass, donkey*
asinus, -ī, m., *ass, donkey*
aspiciō, -ere, -spexī, -spectum, *to look at*

assidō, assidere, assēdī, *to sit down, take a seat*
assiduus, -a, -um, *unceasing, restless*
at, conj., *but*
Atellānus, -a, -um, *of or from Atella*
athlēta, -ae, m., *athlete*
auctiō, -iōnis, f., *public sale, auction*
audiō, -īre, -īvī, -ītum, *to hear*
Augustus, -a, -um, *of August*
aura, -ae, f., *breeze*
aurum, -ī, n., *gold*
aut, conj., *or; otherwise, or else*
avē, int., *greetings!*
axungia, -ae, f., *hog's fat*

B

balneum, -ī, n. *bath*
barbarus, -ī, m., *uncivilized person, barbarian*
basis, -is, f., *stand*
bellus, -a, -um, *fine, excellent; pretty, handsome*
bene, adv., *well*
bēta, -ae, f., *beet*
bibō, -ere, -ī, *to drink*
bis, adv., *twice*
Bompeiiānus, -a, -um, see **Pompēiānus, -a, -um**
bonus, -a, -um, *of good standing; good; gracious* (of gods)
brassica, -ae, f., *cabbage*
Brundisium, -ī, n., *Brundisium*

C

cacātor, -ōris, m., *defecator*
caccabus, -ī, m., *cooking-pot*
cacō, -āre, -āvī, -ātum, *to defecate*
cadaver, -is, m., *corpse*
cadō, -ere, cecidī, cāsum, *to fall, collapse*
caelātor, -ōris, m., *engraver*
caelum, -ī, n., *sky, heaven*
caleō, -ēre, -uī, *to be warm or hot*
calidus, -a, -um, *hot*
calos, int., *hurrah*
Campānus, -a, -um, *of Campania;* m., *inhabitant of Campania*
candēlābrum, -ī, n., *candle-holder*
canō, -ere, cecinī, *to sing*
capela, see **capella**
capella, -ae, f., *she-goat*
Caprātīna, -ae, adj. f., *Capratina* (the epithet under which Juno was worshipped on the *Nōnae Caprātīnae*)
caput, -itis, n., *head*
carmen, -inis, n., *spell*
cārus, -a, -um, *beloved, dear, valued*
castra, -ōrum, n., *military camp*
caupō, -ōnis, m., *shopkeeper; innkeeper*
caveō, -ēre, cāvī, cautum, *to beware, be on guard*
cavō, -āre, -āvī, -ātum, *to make hollow, hollow out*
cēna, -ae, f., *dinner*
cēnaculum, -ī, n., *attic*
cēnō, -āre, -āvī, -ātum, *to dine, have dinner*
cēra, -ae, f., *writing-tablet coated with wax*
cerebrum, -ī, *the brain*
cēterus, -a, -um, *the rest of, the remaining part of*
ceturia [= centuria], -ae, f., *gladiatorial troop; a century (military unit of 100 soldiers)*
Circē, -ēs, f., *Circe*
citō, adv., *quickly, soon*
citrā, prep. + acc., *on this side of*
cīvis, cīvis, m., *citizen*

cliēns, -entis, m., *client* (a person who attaches himself to one of greater political power or influence)
coco [= coquus], -ī, , m., *cook*
coepī, -isse, -tum, *to begin*
cohors, cohortis, f., *cohort*
coiux [= coniūnx], -iugis, m., *partner in marriage*
collēga, -ae, m., *partner, colleague*
colligō, -ere, collēgī, collēctum, *to pick up, collect*
colliquium, -ī, n., *gutter, drain*
colōnia, -ae, f., *colony, settlement*
colōnus, -ī, m., *colonist*
comisereor, -ērī, -itus, *to show pity*
comitium, -ī, n., *a place of assembly*; pl., *election*
commodō, -āre, -āvī, -ātum, *to provide*
commodum, -ī, n., *convenience*
concors, -cordis, adj., *in harmony*
condiscō, -ere, -didicī, *to learn thoroughly*
condō, -ere, -idī, -itum, *to bottle for keeping*
conductor, -ōris, m., *lessee, renter*
conlēga, see **collēga**
cōnsēnsus, -ūs, m., *agreement, general concensus of opinion*
cōnsul, cōnsulis, m., *consul*
cōnsentiō, -īre, -sēnsī, -sēnsum, *to agree, be in agreement*
cōnservō, -āre, -āvī, -ātum, *to preserve*
cōnservus, -ī, m., *fellow slave*
Cōnstantia Nuceria, -ae, f., *Constantia Nuceria*, see **Nuceria**
cōnsul, -is, m., *consul*
contemnō, -ere, -tempsī, -temptum, *to disregard, neglect*
contingō, -ere, -tigī, -tactum, *to be granted to* (+ dat. and inf.)
continuus, -a, -um, *consecutive*
conveniō, -īre, -vēnī, -ventum, *to come together, meet up*
convīva, -ae, m., *a table companion, guest*
cōpia, -ae, f., *opportunity*
cōpō, -ōnis, m., see **caupō**
cōpōnia, -ae, f., *innkeeper, landlady*
coquō, -ere, coxī, coctum, *to cook by boiling, baking or roasting*
cor, cordis, n., *heart*
corōna, -ae, f., *victory crown*
corpus, corporis, n., *body*
costa, -ae, f., *rib*
cotidiānus, -a, -um, *everyday*
crēdō, -ēre, -didī, -ditum, *to believe*
crux, -ucis, f., *cross*
cubiculārius, -ī, m., *servant of the bed chamber*
cum, prep. + acc./abl.., *with*
cum, conj., *when, since, whenever*
cumularis, cumularis, cumulare, ???
cūnctus, -a, -um, *whole, all, every*
cupīdō, -inis, f., *desire*
cupidē, adv., *eagerly*
cupidus, -a, -um, *with eagerness*
cupiō, cupīre, cupiī or **cupīvī, cupītum**, *to desire, wish for*
cūrō, -āre, -āvī, -ātum, *to care about*
currō, -ere, cucurrī, cursum, *to run; to flow swiftly*

D

dē, prep. + abl., *down from, from concerning, about*
dea, -ae, f., *goddess*
dēalbātor, -ōris, m., *whitewasher*

dēalbō, -āre, -āvī, -ātum, *to whitewash, whiten*
dēbeō, -ēre, -uī, -itum, *ought, should* + inf.
dēbilitō, -āre, -āvī, -ātum, *to weaken*
December, -bris, -bre, *of December*
decimus, -a, -um, *tenth*
dēcipiō, -ere, -cēpī, -ceptum, *to deceive, mislead, trick*
dēcrēscō, -ēre, -crēvī, -crētum, *to wane*
decuria, -ae, f., *group, gang (of 10 men)*
decus, -oris, n., *glory*
dēdicātiō, -ōnis, f., *ceremonial dedication*
dēdūcō, dēdūcere, dēdūxī, dēductum, *to bring, escort, show into; subtract from*
dēfēnsor, -ōris, m., *protector, defendor, champion*
dēferō, -ferre, -tulī, lātum, *to bring, carry*
dēgō, -ere, *to spend (one's life)*
dēleō, -ēre, -ēvī, -ētum, *to expunge, efface, destroy*
dēnārius, -ī, m., *denarius* (a silver coin)
dēsertus, -a, -um, *deserted, uninhabited*
dēsīderō, -āre, -āvī, -ātum, *to long for, desire*
deus, ī, m., *deity, god*
diārium, -ī, n., *daily ration of food*
dīcō, dīcere, dīxī, dictum, *to say, tell*
dictō, -āre, -āvī, -ātum, *to recite*
diēs, diēī, m., *day;* **diēs Sāturnī**, *the day of Saturn*, the seventh day of the week
dignus, -a, -um, *worthy*
dīlātiō, -ōnis, f., *postponement, delay*
dīligō, -ere, -lēxī, -lectus, *to love, hold dear*
dipundium, -ī, *a sum of two pennies*
discēdō, -ere, -cessī, -cessum, *to split up, separate*
discēns, -entis, m., *apprentice, trainee*
discō, -ere, didicī, *to learn*
dissignātor, -ōris, m., *official who assigned seats in theatre (and amphitheatre ?)*
diū, adv., *for a long time*
dō, dare, dedī, datum, *to give; hand over, deliver*
doceō, -ēre, -uī, doctum, *to teach*
doctus, -a, -um, *educated*
doleō, -ēre, -uī, *to feel grief*
dolor, -ōris, m., *grief*
dominus, -ī, m., *master, owner; manager*
domna, -ae, f., *mistress*
domnus, -ī, m., see **dominus**
domus, -ūs, f., *town house; residence*
domus, -ī, m., see **dominus**
dormiēns, dormientis, m., *idler*
dormiō, -īre, -īvī or **-iī, -ītum**, *to sleep, be idle*
dulcis, -is, -e, *dear, cherished, agreeable, delightful*
dum, conj., *while, so long as*
duo, dua, duo, *two*
dūrō, -āre, -āvī, -ātum, *to remain unchanged*
dūrus, -a, -um, *hard*
duumvir, duumvirī, m., *duumvir* (holder of highest political office at Pompeii)

E

ego, personal pro., *I*
ēgrōtō, -āre, -āvī, -ātum, see **aegrōtō**
Eidus, -ium, f., see **Īdūs**
Elephantus, -ī, m., *Elephant*, name of an inn
emboliārius, -ī, m., *entertainer who performs at interludes between theatrical performances; clown, buffoon*
emō, emere, ēmī, ēmptum, *to buy*
ēmptor, -ōris, m., *buyer, purchaser, customer*
eō, adv., *in addition*
eō, īre, iī, itum, *to go, leave, depart*
equa, -ae, f., *mare*
eques, equitis, m., *horseman*
equester (-tris), -is, -e, *fit for a knight* (member of the **eques**)
essedārius, -ī, m., *one who fights from a war-chairot* (a type of gladiator)
et, conj., *and, also.* **et . . . et**, conj., *both . . . and*
etiam, particle, *now, yet, still*
ēveniō, -īre, -vēnī, -ventum, *to turn out*
ex or **ē**, prep. + abl., *from, out of; according to*
exclūdō, -ere, -clūsī, -clūsum, *to shut out, exclude*
excutiō, -ere, excussī, excussum, *to shake*
eximō, -ere, -ēmī, -ēmtum, *to take out*
exrogō, -āre, -āvī, -ātum, *to expend private money*

F

facilis, -e, *easy*
faciō, facere, fēcī, factum, *to cause to become; to bring it about, cause it to happen (that); to be sure to; to make*
faenum, -ī, n., *hay*
Falernus, -a, -um, *Falernian*
fallō, -ere, fefellī, falsum, *to lead (someone) into trouble*
familia, -ae, f., *gladiatorial troop*
fascia, -ae, f., *head-band or breast-band*
fateor, -ērī, fassus, *to admit as true, confess*
fatus, -a, -um, *silly, foolish, idiotic*
faveō, -ēre, fāvī, fautum, *to act in support of*
fēlīcitās, -itātis, f., *good fortune, good luck*
fēlīciter, adv., *good luck*
fēlīx, -īcis, adj., *lucky, blessed, fortunate*
feriō, -īre, *to strike down, kill*
feritās, -tātis, f., *fierceness, savageness*
ferō, ferre, tulī, lātum, *to give, provide, offer*
ferreus, -a, -um, *made of iron*
ferrum, -ī, *iron*
fidēs, fideī, f., *good faith, reliability, trust*
fīgō, fīgere, fīxī, fīxum, *to fasten*
fīlia, -ae, f., *daughter*
fīlius, -ī, m., *son*
fīnis, fīnis, gen. pl., **fīnium**, m., *boundary, limit*
fīō, fierī, factus sum, irreg., *to become, be made, be done, happen; to be elected*
flāmen, -inis, m., *priest* (applied to priests of living or deceased emperors)
flamma, -ae, f., *flame*

flōreō, -ēre, -uī, *to enjoy good fortune, prosper; to be in the bloom of youth*
fōns, fontis, f., *bath*
fōrma, -ae, f., *beauty*
forās, adv., *outside*
forte, adv., *by any chance*
fortis, -e, *strong, brave*
fortūna, -ae, f., *fortune* (good or bad)
frangō, -ere, frēgī, fractum, *to break, shatter, smash*
frāter, -tris, m., *brother*
frida, -ae, f., *cold water*
frūgī, indecl. adj., *honest*
frūnīscor, -ī, frūnītus sum, *to enjoy* (+ acc. or abl.)
frūstrā, adv., *in vain*
fugiō, fugere, fūgī, *to flee*
fullō, -ōnis, m., *fuller, launderer*
fulminārium, -ī, n., *incense-burner*
fundus, -ī, m., *farm, country estate*
fūr, fūris, m., *thief*
furfur, -is, m., *bran*
fūrunculus, -ī, m., *small-time crook, pilferer, petty thief*
fustis, fustis, m, *club*

G

gemma, -ae, *seal or signet* (in a ring)
gemmārius, -ī, m., *jeweler*
genetrīx, -trīcis, f., *mother, producer*
genitālis, -is, -e, *connected with one's birth*
gēns, gentis, gen. pl., **gentium**, f., *family, clan*
gerō, gerere, gessī, gestum, *to carry, wear; bear; administer, conduct, manage*
glaber, -bra, -brum, *bald, hairless*
gladiātōrius, -a, -um, *gladiatorial*
glōria, -ae, f., *praise, honor, glory*
grātīs, adv., *without payment, for free*
gustō, -āre, -āvī, -ātum, *to partake of*
gutus, -ī, m., *flask*

H

habeō, -ēre, -uī, -itum, *to have, hold*
habiō, see **habeō**
habitō, -āre, -āvī, -ātum, *to live, dwell*
hāc, adv., *here; thus far*
haēna, -ae, f., *bronze vessel*
hama, -ae, f., *water-bucket*
hamula, -ae, f., *small bucket*
heic, see **hīc**
hic, haec, hoc, *this, the latter*
hīc, adv., *here*
homō, hominis, m., *man*
honerāta, see **onerō**
honestus, -a, -um, *regarded with honor or respect*
honōs, honōris, m., *honor, political office*
hōra, -ae, f., *hour*
hospes, -itis, m., *guest, visitor*
hospitium, -ī, n. *lodgings*
hūc, adv., *to this place*

I

iaciō, -ere, -uī, iactum, *to throw*
iam, adv., *now, already*
iānitor, -ōris, m., d*oor-keeper*
iānua, -ae, f., *door*
Iānuārius, -a, -um, *of January*
īc, see **hīc**
īdem, eadem, idem, *the same*
idicium, -ī, n., *pronoucement*
Īdūs, -ium, f., *Ides*

ignis, ignis, m., *fire*
ille, illa, illud, *that; he, she, it; the former*
impēnsa, -ae, f., *cost, expenditure, expense*
imperātor, imperātōris, m., *commander, emperor*
imperium, -ī, n., *empire, power*
in, prep. + abl., *in, on, among*
in, prep. + acc., *into, against*
inānis, -is, -e, *empty*
inaurēs, -ium, f. pl., *ear-rings*
indidem, adv., *from the same place*
īnfēlīx, -īcis, adj., *unlucky, unfortunate*; n. pl., *bad luck, curses*
ingenuus, -a, -um, *inborn*
inimīca, -ae, f., *enemy*
innocentia, -ae, f., *integrity, uprightness*
inperātor, -ōris, m., see **imperātor, imperātoris**, m.
īnstrūmentum, -ī, n., *equipment, tools*
īnsula, -ae, f., *apartment block*
inter, prep. + acc., *between, among*
intrō, adv., *inside*
invictus, -a, -um, *unconquered, undefeated*
invideō, -ēre, -vīdī, -vīsum, *be jealous of*
invidiōsus, -a, -um, *odious, invidious; jealous.*
invidiōsē, adv., *with ill will*
ipse, ipsa, ipsum, *himself, herself, itself, themselves; the great one;* **ipsa**, f., *mistress*
īra, -ae, f., *anger*
īrātus, -a, -um, *angry*
is, ea, id, *he, she, it; this, that*
Īsiācī, -ōrum, m., *worshipers in the cult of Isis*
isse, see **ipse**
ita, adv., *thus, so, in this way, in such a way*
itaque, adv., *and so*
item, adv., *also*
iūdex, -icis, m., *arbiter*
iūdicium, -ī, n., *decisions*
iūmentum, -ī, n. , *team of mules*
Iūnius, -a, -um, *of June*
Iūpiter (Iuppiter), Iovis, m., *Jupiter*
iūs, iūris, n., *right, justice, duty*; **iūrē dīcundō** dat. sg. neut. *for declaring the law* (**iūrē** is an archaic dative singular form for **iūrī**)
iuvenis, iuvenis, m., *young man* (adult male up to the age of 45)

K

Kalendae, -ārum, f., *Kalends*

L

labor, -ōris, m., *work, labor, task*
laedō, -ere, laesī, laesum, *to damage, disfigure*
lanifricārius, -ī, m., *wool-worker*
lanternārius, -ī, m., *lantern-carrier*
Lar, Laris, m., *Lar* (tutelary god of hearth and home)
latrunculārius, -ī, m., *player of a board game*
laxus, -a, -um, *wide open*
lector, -ōris, m., *reader*
lectus, -ī, m. *bed, couch*
lēgitimus, -a, -um, *prescribed by usage, custom; proper*
legō, -ere, lēgī, lēctus, *read*
levis, -is, -e, *gentle, light*
līber, lībera, līberum, *free*
līberī, -ōrum, m. pl., *children*
lībertus, -ī, m., *freedman*

libēs [= **libēns**], **-entis**, *willing*
lībra, -ae, f., *a balance, pair of scales; a pound* (measure of weight)
licet, -ēre, licuit, *it is permitted, one may*
lignārius, -ī, *worker or dealer in wood*
lingō, -ere, līnxī, līnctum, *to lick*
locō, -āre, -āvī, -ātum, *to let for rent, to lease*
locum, -ī, n., see **locus, -ī**
locus, -ī, m., *rank, position, precedence; place;* n. in pl., *places*
lōrum, -ī, n., (pl.) *reins*
lūcerna, -ae, f., *lamp*
lucrum, -ī, n., *gain, profit*
lucubrātōrium, -ī, n., *light stand*
lūdō, -ere, lūsī, lūsum, *to gamble*
lūdus, -ī, m., *school, game;* pl., *games*
lūna, -ae, f., *moon; new moon;* **ad lūnam**, *by moonlight*
lumbus, -ī, m., (pl.) *hips, loins*
lytrum, -ī, n., *wash-basin*

M

magis, adv., *more, to a greater extent*
magister, magistrī, m., *schoolmaster, master, captain*
maior, maior, maius, gen., **maiōris**, *bigger.* **maiōrēs, maiōrum**, m. pl., *ancestors*
Māius, -a, -um, *of May*
mala, of uncertain meaning (see I, 2, 59)
mālō, mālle, māluī, irreg., *to prefer*
malum, -ī, n., *evil-doing, misdeed, trouble*
malus, -a, -um, *painful, unpleasant, bad*
Mamiānus, -a, -um, *belonging to Mamius*
maneō, -ēre, māsī [= **mānsī**], **mānsum**, *to stay*
manuplus, -ī, m., *bundle*
manus, -ūs, f., *hand*
marmor, -oris, n., *marble basin*
matella, -ae, f., *chamberpot*
mathēmaticus, -ī, m., *mathematician*
maximus, -a, -um, *biggest, greatest, very great, very large*
maxumus, -a, -um, see **maximus, -a, -um**
medācium [= **mendācium**], **-ī**, n., *lie, falsehood*
medicō, -āre, -āvī, -ātum, *to treat, give medical treatment to*
melius, melius, melior, gen. **meliōris**, *better*
memoria, -ae, f., *memory*
mendāx, -ācis, adj., *untruthful, lying*
menedemerumenus, of unknown meaning (nonsense?)
mereō, -ēre, -uī, -itum, *to deserve;* **bene mereō**, *to deserve well*
meritō, adv., *deservedly*
meritum, -ī, n., *meritorious service*
mercēs, -ēdis, f., *payment*
merum, -ī, n., *wine unmixed with water*
meus, -a, -um, *my, mine*
mīlis [= **mīles**], **mīlitis**, m., *soldier*
mīlitō, -āre, -āvī, -ātum, *to serve as a soldier*
milium, ī, n., *millet*
mille, indecl. n., *thousand;* **mīlia, -ium**, pl., *thousands*
mingō, -ere, mīxī, mictum, *to urinate*
minimus, -a, -um, *smallest*

mittō, -ere, mīsī, missum, *to send; to pardon, dismiss from service*
modius, -ī, m., *measure*
modo, adv., *a little while ago*
molestē, adv., *in a distressing manner;* **molestē ferre**, *to be troubled*
mollis, -is, -e, *soft*
moneō, -ēre, -uī, -itum, *to warn*
mōns, montis, f., *mountain*
mora, -ae, f., *waste of time*
morātor, -ōris, m., *loiterer*
morior, -ī, *to die*
moror, -ārī, -ātus, *to stop, pause on one's way*
mors, mortis, gen. pl., **mortium**, f., *death*
mortus, see **mortuus**
mortuus, -a, -um, *dead*
mōs, mōris, n., pl., *manners*
mōstrō [= mōnstrō], -āre, -āvī, -ātum, *to show the way, give directions*
moveō, -ēre, mōvī, mōtum, *to disturb*
mūliō, -ōnis, m., *muleteer, mule-driver*
multō, adv., *by far, much*
multus, -a, -um, *many*
mūlus, -ī, m., *mule*
munerārius, -ī, m., *a sponsor of gladiatorial or other public shows*
mūnus, mūneris, n., *gladiatorial show;* pl., *games*
mūrus, -ī, m., *city-wall, boundary wall*
muscella, -ae, f., *little fly*
mūtō, -āre, -āvī, -ātum, *to transform, change*

N

nam, sent. part., *for*
nāscor, -ī, nātus, *to be born*
nāvis, -is, f., *ship*
nē, conj. + subjunctive, *not to, so that . . . not*
nec, neg., *not*
necese [= necesse], indecl. adj., *necessary*
nēcuisma, superl. of **nēquam**
nēmō, -inis, m., *no one*
nēquam, indecl. adj., *worthless*
Nerōniānus, -a, -um, *Neronian* (from the gladiatorial school of Nero)
nesciō, -īre, -iī, -ītum, *not to know*
nīl, see **nīhil**
nihil, n. indec., *nothing*
niteō, -ēre, -uī, *to be radiant*
nox, noctis, f., *night*
Nola, -ae, f., *Nola* (city in Campania)
Nolānus, -a, um, *of Nola*
nōlō, nōlle, nōluī, *to be unwilling, not to want to*
nōmen, nōminis, n., *name*
nōn, neg., *not*
Nōnae, -ārum, f., *Nones*
nōngentī, -ae, -a, *nine hundred*
noster, nostra, nostrum, *our*
November, -bris, -bre, *of November*
Nūceria, -ae, f., *Nuceria* (town in Campania)
Nūcerīnus, -a, -um, *of or from Nuceria;* m., *inhabitant of Nuceria*
Nūcherīnus, -a, -um, see **Nūcerīnus, -a, -um**
nugās, -ācis, adj., *of no consequence*

nūllus, -a, -um, *no, none*
numerus, -ī, m., *number*
nūmen, -inis, n., *divinenature, godhead*
nummus, -ī, m., *coin*, often a *sesterce* (a denomination of Roman coinage)
nunc, adv., *now*
nundinae, -ārum, f. pl. *market-day (held every ninth day)*
nunquam [= numquam], adv., *never*

O

ob, prep. + acc., *because of, on account of*
obdūcō, -ere, -dūxī, -ductum, *to close*
obiurgō, -āre, -āvī, -ātum, *to reprimand, find fault with*
occupō, -āre, -āvī, -ātum, *to seize, take possession of*
Ōceanus, -ī, m., *ocean*
Octāviānus, -a, -um, *Octavian* (name of a gladiatorial school)
octāvus, -a, -um, *eighth*
oleum, -ī, n., *olive-oil*
ōlim, adv., *once*
olīva, -ae, f., *olive*
olla, -ae, f., *cooking pot or jar*
Olyxis, -is, m., *Odysseus*
omnipotēs [= omnipotēns], -entis, adj., *all-powerful*
omnis, -is, -e, *all, the whole, every, each*
onerō, -āre, -āvī, -ātum, *to load with goods or cargo*
operārius, -ī, m., *workman*
operculum, -ī, n., *panel for walls*
opordet [= oportet], -ēre, -uit, *it is proper, right*
oppidum, -ī, n., *town*
optimus, -a, -um, *best*
optumē [= optimē], adv, *best*
optumus, see **optimus**
ōra [= hōra], -ae, f., *hour*
ōra, -ae, f., *distant land*
ōrdō, ōrdinis, m., *town council, senate or ruling body of a municipality*
ōrō, ōrāre, ōrāvī, ōrātum, *to beseech, plead*
ōs, ōris, n., *mouth*
ōtiōsus, -a, -um, *idle, at leisure*
osculum, -ī, n., *kiss*

P

palea, -ae, f., *chaff of corn*
palim, adv., *again*
pallium, -ī, n., *cloak*
pālus, -ī, m., *wooden post, stake*
pānis, pānis, m., *bread*
pār, paris, n., *set of two, pair*
Paridiānī, -ōrum, m. pl., *the troop of the pantomime Paris*
pariēns [= pariēs], -etis, f., *wall*
pariō, -ere, peperī, partum, *to give birth*
parma, -ae, f., *small, round shield*
pater, patris, m., *father; saviour, protector*
patior, patī, passus, *to suffer, endure, permit*
patria, -ae, f., *country, homeland, native land*
pauper, -ī, m., *poor man*
peccō, -āre, -āvī, -ātum, *to make a mistake*
pectus, -oris, n., *breast, chest*
pecūnia, -ae, f., *money*
pelvis, -is, f., *shallow bowl*
pereō, perīre, perī [= periī], peritum, *to vanish, dissappear; to die, perish*

pergula, -ae, f., *attachment to building used for trading* (sometimes constructed as an upper storey)
periō, see **pereō**
permissus, -ūs, m., *authorization*
perna, -ae, f., *ham*
pernīs, -īcis, adj., *agile, swift, speedy*
perpetuō, adv., *continuously, permanently, indefintely*
perpetuus, -a, -um, *lasting, permanent*
persolvō, persolvere, persolvī, persolūtum, *to give/pay out*
pertundō, -ere, -tudī, -tūsum, *to bore a hole through*
petō, -ere, -īvī, -ītum, *to seek to obtain*
Petūcūsānus, -a, -um, *of or from Pithecusa*; m., *inhabitant of Pithecusa*
Phoebē, -ēs, f., *Phoebe* (goddess of the moon)
pietās, -ātis, f., *dutiful respect*
pilicrepus, -ī, m., of uncertain meaning, perhaps *ballplayer, scorer*
pingō, -ere, pīnxī [also spelled **pīnxsī], pictum**, *to draw, paint*
pīstor, pīstōris, m., *miller, baker*
plausus, -ūs, m., *applause, approval*
plēnus, -a, -um, *full*
plōstrārius, -ī, m., *wagoneer*
plūs, plūris, n., *more*
plūrimus, -a, -um, *most enthusiastic, greatest*
poena, -ae, f., *punishment*
pomārius, -ī, m., *fruit-vendor*
Pompeī, -ōrum, m. pl., *Pompeii*
Pompēiānus, -a, -um, *of Pompeii*; m.. pl. *people, inhabitants of Pompeii*
pondō, adv., *in weight, by weight*
pōnō, pōnere, posuī, postum [= positum], *to put, place; deposit*
pōns, pontis, m., *bridge*
Popeī, -ōrum, see **Pompeī, -ōrum**
populus, -ī, m., *people*
porta, -ae, f., *gate*
possum, posse, potuī, irreg., *to be able; can*
post, prep. + acc., *after*
posteā, adv., *afterward*
postulō, -āre, -āvī, -ātum, *to demand*
pote, indecl. adj., *able*
praedium, -ī, n., *property*
praesēns, -entis, adj., *present*
praetōriānus, -ā, -um, *praetorian*
premō, -ere, pressī, pressum, *to press, push*
prēndō, -ere, prēndī, prēnsum, *to take hold of, grasp, seize, apprehend*
prēsē(ns), -entis, adj., *present*; cf. **praesēns**
prīdiē, adv. , *on the day before*
prīmipīlāris, -is, m., *senior centurion of the legion* (centurion commanding first century of first cohort)
prīmus, -a, -um, *first; next*
prīvātus, -a, -um, *private*
prīnceps, prīncipis, *leading*
prīnceps, prīncipis, m., *emperor, leader, leading citizen*
prō, prep. + acc. or abl., *for, on behalf of, as*
probē, adv., *in a manner worthy of approval*
probitās, -itātis, f., *moral integrity, uprightness, honesty*
probō, -āre, -āvī, -ātum, *to approve of*

probus, -a, -um, *having upright character, honest, virtuous*
prōcūrō, -āre, -āvī, -ātum, *to take care of*
prōcūrātor, -ōris, m., *person in charge of gladiatorial school*
proelior, -ārī, -ātus, *to fight*
proficiscor, -ī, -fectus, *to set out, depart*
prōgredior, -ī, -gressus, *to go forward*
properō, -āre, -āvī, -ātum, *to be in a hurry*
propiteus, -a, -um, see **propitius, -a, -um**
propitius, -a, -um, *favorably disposed*
propytius, -a, -um, see **propitius, -a, -um**
prōsum, prōdesse, prōfuī, irreg., *to be advantageous, beneficial*
prōvocātor, -ōris, m., *provocator* (a type of gladiator)
pūblicus, -a, -um, *public*
pudor, pudōris, m., *sense of propriety, decency, scrupulousness*
puella, -ae, f., *sweetheart; young woman*
puer, -ī, m., *servant-boy*
pugnō, -āre, -āvī, -ātum, *to fight*
pulsō, -āre, -āvī, -ātum, *to knock*
pungō, -ere, pupugī, punctum, *to goad*
pūpa, -ae, f., *girl*
pusillum, -ī, n., *a little bit*
Puteolānus, -a, -um, *of or from Puteoli*
Puteolī, -ōrum, m. pl., *Puteoli* (a town on the Campanian coast near Naples, modern Pozzuoli)
Putiolānus, -a, -um, see **Puteolānus, -a, -um**
putō, -āre, -āvī, -ātum, *to consider (to be), to regard (as)*

Q

quā, rel. adv., *wherever*
quaerō, -ere, -īvī, -ītum, *to seek after*
quaestor, -ōris, m., *quaestor*
quam, adv., *than, as*
quantus, -a, -um, *how big? how much?*
quārē, adv., *why*
quārtus, -a, -um, *fourth*
quater, adv., *four times*
quatuor [= quattuor], indecl. num., *four*
quattus, indec., *sum of four pennies*
-que, enclitic conj., *and*
quī, quae, quod, rel. pron., *who, which, that;* indef. pron., *anyone, anything*
quīnque, num., *five*
quīnquennālis, -e, *quinquennial, that takes place every five years*
quīntus, -a, -um, *fifth*
quis, qua/quae, quid, indef. pron. and adj., *anyone, anything; some, any*
quis, quid, *who?, what?* **nē quis, quid**, *lest anyone, anything*
quisquam, quisquam, quicquam, *anyone, anything*
quisque, quaeque, quodque, adj., *every, each*
quisquis, quidquid, indef. rel. pron., *whoever, whatever*
quit, rel. adv., *why*
quō, rel. adv., *to which place*
quoad, rel. adv., *for as long as, while*
quod, conj., *because*

quoque, adv., *also*

R

recēns, -entis, adj., *recent*
recipiō, -ere, -cēpī, -ceptum, *to welcome, recieve, allow to enter*
rēctē, adv., *(really) well*
recūsō, -āre, -āvī, -ātum, *to protest, object to*
reddō, -ere, -didī, -ditum, *to produce*; refl., *to return oneself to*
redeō, redīre, redī [= rediī], reditum, *to return, come back*
referō, referre, rettulī, relātum, *to bring back*
rēgīna, -ae, f., *queen*
regnō, -āre, -āvī, -ātum, *to rule, hold sway*
relinquō, -ere, relīquī, relictus, *to leave behind; disregard*
reliquus, -a, -um, *rest of, remaining*
rēs, reī, f., *thing, matter, situation, affair; product*
rēs pūblica, reī pūblicae, f., *republic, the state*
restituō, -ere, -stituī, -stitūtum, *to restore*
rētiārius, -ī, m., *a net-thrower* (a type of gladiator)
retineō, -ēre, -uī, -tentum, *to hold fast, prevent from escaping, restrain*
rhetor, -ōris, m., *rhetorician* (one who teaches public speaking)
rhetoricos, ī, m., *a teacher of rhetoric*
rīvālis, -is, m., *rival*
rīxō, -āre, *to quarrel violently or noisily*
rogō, rogāre, rogāvī, rogātum, *to ask (someone) to elect (someone); entreat, beg*
Rōma, -ae, f., *Rome*
Rōmānus, -a, -um, *Roman*
Rōmulus, -ī, m., *Romulus, legendary founder of Rome*
rota, -ae, f., *wheel, potter's wheel*
ruīna, -ae, f., (pl.) *ruins*

S

sacer, sacra, sacrum, *sacred*
Saliniēnsis, -is, m., *inhabitant of Salinium* (a neighborhood in Pompeii located near the Porta Ercolano)
salūs, -ūtis, f. *personal safety; greeting, salutation*
salvus, -a, -um, *in good health*
sānctus, -a, -um, *sacrosanct, scrupulous, upright*
Sarnus, -ī, m., *Sarno river*
Sāturnus, ī, m., *Saturn* (an ancient Roman god); see **diēs**
saxsum [= saxum], -ī, n., *rock, stone*
scaena, -ae, f., *performance on the stage*
scaenicī, -ōrum, m. pl., *theatrical shows*
scāla, -ae, f. *ladder*
scapheola, -ae, f., *small tub*
sciō, -īre, -īvī, -ītum, *to know*
scrībō, scrībere, scrīpsī, scrīptum, *to paint, to write*
scrīptor, -ōris, m., *writer*
Scythia, -ae, f., *Scythia*
sē, reflexive pron., *himself, herself, oneself, itself, themselves*
secundus, -a, -um, *second*
sēdēs, -is, f., *home*
sei, see **sī**
seiquis, see **sī**, **quis**

sella, -ae, f., *seat, chair*
sēmis, -issis, m., *one half of an as*
sēmuncia, -ae, f., *saddle-bag*
semper, adv., *always*
sententia, -ae, f., *opinion*
sentiō, -īre, sēnsī, sēnsum, *to experience*
September, -bris, -bre, *of September*
septimus, -a, -um, *seventh*
sera, -ae, f., *door-bolt*
sēribibī, -ōrum, m., *late-drinkers* (name of a drinking-club?)
serus, see **servus**
servō, -āre, -āvī, -ātum, *to recover, regain*
servos, see **servus**
servus, -ī, m., *slave*
sēstertius, -ī, m., *sesterce* (a denomination of Roman coinage)
sextus, -a, -um, *sixth*
sī, conj., *if*
sīc, adv., *in this way, so*
sīg, adv., see **sīc**
signō, -āre, -āvī, -ātum, *to affix a seal to* (a letter or document)
sine, prep. + abl., *without*
sīparium, -ī, n., *curtain used as backdrop for mimic performances*
sīquī, see **sī** and **quī**
sīquis, see **sī, quis**
sitiō, -īre, *to be thirsty*
socius, -ī, m., *companion*
sodālis, sodālis, m., *member of a society/fraternity/priesthood*
sōl, sōlis, m., *sun*
solitus, -a, -um, *usual, accustomed, normal*
solvō, -ere, -vī, -ūtum, *to fulfill*
sōlus, -a, -um, *alone*
somniō, -īre, -īvī, -ītum, *to day-dream*
somnum, -ī, n., *sleep*
soror, -ōris, f., *sister*
spargō, -ere, sparsī, sparsum, *to scatter, sprinkle*
sparsiō, -ōnis, f., *the scattering of largess to audiences in the amphitheatre*
spectāclum [= spectāculum], -ī, *show, spectacle*
spectō, -āre, -āvī, -ātum, *to watch*
Stabiānus, -a, -um, *of or belonging to Stabiae*; as m., *the people of Stabiae*
stāmin{i} [= stamen], staminis, n., *vertical threads in a loom, the warp*
stecus, see **stercus**
stercorārius, -ī, m., *a person who hauls manure, dung*
stercus, -oris, n., *dung, manure, excrement*
stō, -āre, stetī, statum, *to stand*
strigilis, -is, f., *scraper, strigil*
suāvis, -is, -e, *delightful, charming*
su, sub, prep. + abl., *under, beneath; under the command of*
succurrō, -ere, -ī, -cursum, *to hasten to the assistance of*
sufferō, -ferre, -tulī, -lātum, *to endure*
sum, esse, fuī, irreg., *to be*
summa, -ae, f., *total number/amount*
summus, summa, summum, *greatest, very great, highest*
superus, -a, -um, *dwelling in heaven*; m. pl., *gods*
suppositīcius, -a, -um, *substitute*
supsteneō [= sustineō], -ēre, -uī, -tentum, *to support*
surdus, -a, -um, *unresponsive*
surgō, -ere, -rēxī, -rēctum, *to get up, rise to one's feet*

suspendō, -ere, -ī, -sum, *to hang oneself*
suspīrium, -ī, n., *sigh of desire*
sustineō, -ēre, -uī, -tentum, *to endure*
suus, -a, -um, *his, her, one's, its, their (own); his/her beloved* (esp. with personal names)

T

taberna, -ae, f., *an inn*
taedium, -ī, n., *scribbling*
tālis, tālis, tāle, *of such (exceptionally bad/good) character or kind*
tamen, adv., *nevertheless, all the same*
tan [= tam], adv., *so, as*
tantum, -ī, n., *such a quantity, so much*
tēgulum, -ī, f., *roofing*
templum, -ī, n., *temple*
tempus, -oris, n., *time*
teneō, -ēre, -uī, -tum, *to grasp, take hold of, hold fast*
tener, -a, -um, *soft, tender, delicate*
ter, adv., *three times*
tertiō, adv., *for the third time*
textor, -ōris, m., *weaver*
Timniānus, -a, -um, *Timnian*
tīrō, -ōnis, m., *novice*
tōt, indecl. adj., *so many*
Traex, -ācis, m., *Thracian*, a type of gladiator
trāseō [= trānseō], -īre, -iī or -īvī, -itum, *to pass by*
trēs, trēs, tria, *three*
trīcē(n)simus, -a, -um, *thirtieth*
trīcium, -ī, n., *wheat*
trichlīnium, see **triclīnium**
triclīnium, -ī, n., *dining-room*
trīticum, -ī, n., *wheat*
Trōia, -ae, f., *Troy*
tū, pers. pron., *you*
tunica, -ae, f., *tunic*
turba, -ae, f., *throng, mass, crowd*
turma, -ae, f., *troop of mounted gladiators*
tūtō, -āre, *to protect*
tūtor, -ārī, -ātus, *to protect*

U

ubi, rel. adv., *where*
ubīque, adv., *everywhere*
ūllus, -a, -um, *any*
ulula, -ae, f., *owl*
ūnā, adv., *together*
uncus, -ī, m., *hook*
unda, -ae, f., *water*
unde, interrog. adv., *from where; from whom*
ūnicus, -a, -um, *alone, one and olnly*
ūniversus, -a, -um, *the whole of, the entire group of, all*
ūnus, -a, -um, *one*
urciolus [= urceolus], -ī, m., *small jug*
urna, -ae, f., *pitcher, urn*
ūrō, -ere, ussī, ustus, *to consume, destroy by fire*
ursus, -ī, m., *bear*
usce, adv., *right up (to)*; see **usque**
usque, adv., *continuously*
ūsūra, -ae, f., *interest*
ut, conj. + subj., *so that, that, to*
uterque, utraque, utrumque, *each* (of two), *both*
utinam, part. introducing wishes, *how I wish that*

V

valeō, -ēre, -uī, *to be in sound health, be well; farewell!, goodbye!*

valiō, see **valeō**
vedō [vendō], -ere, -idī, -itum, *to sell*
veivō, see **vīvō**
vēlum, -ī, n., *awning*
vēnālis, -is, -e, *for sale*
vēnātiō, vēnātiōnis, f., *animal-hunt; a troop of animal-hunters*
Venerius, -a, -um, *of Venus*
veniō, venīre, vēnī, ventum, *to come, go*
ventus, -ī, m., *wind*
venus, -eris, f., *love*
Venus, -eris, f., *Venus*
venustus, -a, -um, *charming*
vērāx, -ācis, adj., *truthful*
verber, -eris, n., (pl.) *instrument for flogging; lashes*
verbum, -ī, n., *word*
verēcundus, -a, -um, *having a regard for propriety*
vērum, -ī, n., *truth*
vērus, -a, -um, *true*
vespertīnus, -a, -um, *of or belonging to the evening*
vetō, -āre, -uī, -itum, *to forbid, prohibit*
via, -ae, f., *road*
viria, -ae, f., *bracelet*
viātor, -ōris, m., *traveler*
vīcīnus, -ī, m., *neighbor*
victor, victōris, m., *conqueror, victor*
victōria, -ae, f., *victory*
vīcus, -ī, m., *neighborhood*
videō, vidēre, vīdī, vīsum, *to see*
vigilō, -āre, -āvī, -ātum, *to be watchful, alert*
vincō, vincere, vīcī, victum, *to conquer, win*
vīnum, -ī, n., *wine*
violō, -āre, -āvī, -ātum, *to injure*
vir, -ī, m., *man, husband*
vīsō, -ere, -ī, *to go and see*
vīta, -ae, f., *life*
vīvō, vīvere, vīxī, vīctum, *to live*
vīvus, -a, -um, *living*
vōcō, -āre, -āvī, -ātum, *to call*
volō, velle, voluī, irreg., *to wish, want, be willing*
votō, see **vetō**
vōtum, -ī, n., *vow* (made to a god to offer something in return for granting a favor)

Roman Topography and Travel

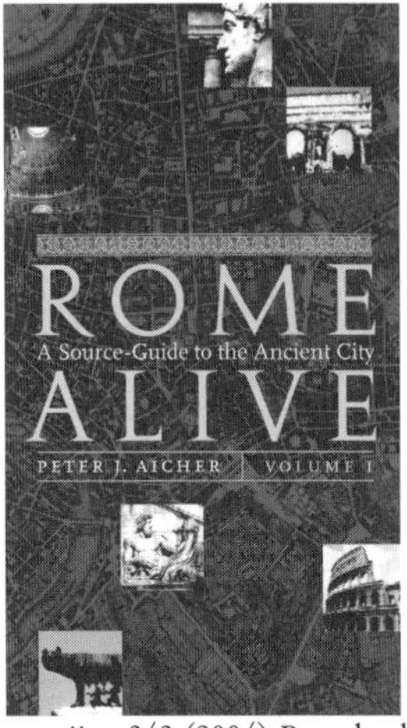

xxxii + 343 (2004) Paperback
ISBN 0-86516-473-8

xxxii + 343 (2004) Paperback
ISBN 0-86516-507-6

An exciting field companion and original-language source-book for navigating Rome's monuments

Rome Alive, Volume I is a one-of-a-kind guide, perfect for every traveler to Rome's ancient city, whether armchair tourist, first-time visitor, or veteran of the city's charms. Through observations (translated into English) of ancient authors, this guide takes the visitor to ancient Rome's key sites in the company of eyewitnesses to Rome's zenith. Aicher's own introductory comments quickly orient the visitor to each site's significance. Photographs, maps, and floor plans abound.

Rome Alive, Volume II is a companion to Volume I, aimed at the scholar-traveler who wants access to the Latin and Greek original sources translated into English in Volume I. This unique original-language guide to ancient Rome's monuments gathers together compelling observations of the ancient authors who witnessed Rome's zenith. Key maps from Volume I are included.

Aicher's guide deserves much praise and is remarkably useful....Anyone wanting to visit the aqueducts from now on must use it;...—one of the greatest achievements of Roman technology

—**James C. Anderson, Jr.**, *The Classical Outlook*

...engaging and well presented, and well illustrated... Of interest to high school teachers as well as to university professors and travelers.

—**Gilbert Lavall**, *University of Masachusetts, Amherst*

Enlivening and fascinating...can serve both the appreciative tourist and the serious student of the ancient world...

—**Robert Rodgers**, *University of Vermont*

Illus., xiii + 183 pp. (1995)
Paperback ISBN 0-86516-282-4
Hardbound ISBN 0-86516-271-9

www.Bolchazy.com